CREATING LIFE BEFORE DEATH

Bernard Phillips
Thomas J. Savage
Andy Plotkin
Neil S. Weiss
Max O. Spitzer

CREATING LIFE BEFORE DEATH

Bernard Phillips
Thomas J. Savage
Andy Plotkin
Neil S. Weiss
Max O. Spitzer

First published in 2020
as part of the Interdisciplinary Social Sciences Book Imprint
http://doi.org/10.18848/978-1-86335-182-9/CGP (Full Book)

BISAC Codes: SOC026000, SEL000000, EDU000000

Common Ground Research Networks
2001 South First Street, Suite 202
University of Illinois Research Park
Champaign, IL
61820

Library of Congress Cataloging-in-Publication Data

Names: Phillips, Bernard S., author.
Title: Creating life before death / Bernard Phillips [and four others].
Description: Champaign, IL : Common Ground Research Networks, 2020. |
 Includes bibliographical references and index. | Summary: "This book
 presents a unique interdisciplinary perspective addressing our double
 crisis of how to live a meaningful life in a world of escalating
 problems. The first two authors are a scholar and a preacher who provide
 social science knowledge combined with stories from the personal
 experiences of a minister-cop. We are joined by a sociologist, an
 economist and a medical social scientist. People have failed to
 understand that the further development of the individual, which we
 center on, is the basis for the continuing evolution of society. Every
 single one of us has awesome intellectual, emotional, and
 problem-solving potentials. We can learn to fulfill them by fully using
 our two most powerful tools: language and the scientific method. They
 can resist bureaucratic conformity that stifles creative innovation and
 interdisciplinary cooperation. Many have claimed that what they are
 doing is changing the world. With no exaggeration, this book actually
 takes basic steps in that direction"-- Provided by publisher.
Identifiers: LCCN 2019047042 (print) | LCCN 2019047043 (ebook) | ISBN
 9781863351805 (hardback) | ISBN 9781863351812 (paperback) | ISBN
 9781863351829 (pdf)
Subjects: LCSH: Social problems. | Quality of life. | Sociology.
Classification: LCC HN18.3 .P485 2020 (print) | LCC HN18.3 (ebook) | DDC
 306--dc23
LC record available at https://lccn.loc.gov/2019047042
LC ebook record available at https://lccn.loc.gov/2019047043

Cover Photo Credit: Phillip Kalantzis-Cope

Table of Contents

Foreword

Jonathan H. Turner

Sociology in the United States today now appears to be overly focused on a set of issues that are manifestations of more fundamental problems in human societies. The present-day emphasis of the discipline on inequalities and injustices experienced by certain categories of individuals is indeed important. But it is an outcome of a more general problem in societies: oppressive stratification and other forms of constraint on human beings. As populations grew during the course of societal development, societies became more complex and demanding, often forcing individuals to subordinate their sense of self to the sociocultural demands that humans had created. With their evolved capacities for constructing the world to which they must adapt, humans ended up building their own social cages that often drains them of their humanity. To organize large populations does require building sociocultural formations, but these do not by necessity need to be so constraining. This is the message of *Creating Life Before Death*: *Humans are not living the life that they can or should be living, given their fundamental nature.*

If we go back to an earlier time in the 20th century, sociology and other disciplines as diverse as clinical psychology, psychoanalytic theory, history, philosophy, and literature were all addressing a broader set of fundamental problems that had also troubled most of the founding figures of sociology—Comte, Marx, Spencer, Durkheim, and Weber. Indeed, sociology was created to understand the problems inhering in the increasing scale of human societies: the bureaucratic organization of social life, the increasing loss of individualism in the face of demands for conformity, the increasing alienation of humans from themselves and the social world, the corruption of democracies, the rise of fascism, the increasing potential for violent revolutions, the spread of warfare into a world-level phenomenon, and a host of "pathologies" inhering in modernity at the level of the individual and the organization of societies.

Marx wanted to liberate humans from the constraints of exploitation; Comte wanted to create sociology to solve not only Marx's problem but all social problems with a new "queen science"; Spencer wanted to preserve the dignity of individuals in complex, differentiated societies by reducing inequalities and concentrations of power in favor of open and free markets where individuals had choices; Durkheim wanted to do much the same while integrating individuals in a common culture and community; and Weber worried about the "steel enclosure" of rational-legal bureaucracies and their effects on humans as persons and individuals, seeing rationalization as a force that creates a disenchanted social universe. Yet, like Weber, Marx, Spencer, and Durkheim, others like Georg Simmel also saw some potential in complex, differentiated societies for reducing constraints and giving individuals freedom to make choices in tune with their needs and desires.

By the mid-20th century, sociologists of varying political orientations (yes, that was once possible in American sociology) saw many of the same problems, whether it be C. Wright Mills' vision in *The Sociological Imagination*, *The Power Elite*, and *White Collar*, Alvin W. Gouldner's conviction that there would be *A Coming Crisis in Western Sociology* that mirrored that in human societies, or Robert Nisbet's concern over the loss of community in his *The Quest for Community*. Outside of sociology in the mid-20th century were similar calls for greater examination of what was happening to individuals in societies, whether it be from the psychoanalytic standpoint of Karen Horney and Erich Fromm, or from literary figures of many stripes, such as Aldous Huxley in *Brave New World* or George Orwell in *Nineteen Eighty-Four*.

These kinds of commentaries on the human condition continue today, but they have lost much of their novelty and their ability to stop and *make us think* about what we, as sentient human beings, are doing to ourselves. In some ways, we have even "externalized" our concerns about society to emotionally safer concerns like the damage being done to the planet's ecosystem and other life forms—almost to the point where we have lost sight of the *great emotional harm that humans are inflicting on themselves*. Indeed, the current concerns over discrimination and inequality are yet another form of externalization by Americans and sociologists, in particular, who focus on the injustices that some have done to others. They are almost forgetting what individuals and their sociocultural creations have done to all humanity more generally. This includes not only racists, sexists, and others who hate some categories of their fellow human beings. It equally bears on sociologists and average citizens who must live in a social universe of constraint that violates what evolved humans need.

I have long shared all of the above concerns, which have been aggravated by the effect of the media and of *media*ted social relations made possible by information technologies. They could potentially be a tool of liberation, but, ironically, seem to have become one more form of sociocultural constraint if not repression of human needs. It perhaps began with radio, but more likely with television, which, comparatively, now seems rather harmful. Our information technologies moved on to the creation of the internet, and then to the advent of cell phones, and their impact on humans. We now have addicted users of cell phones, with many compulsively and somewhat shamelessly presenting themselves to communities of "friends" and "followers" who now have the power to make one's self esteem contingent on their mercurial approval.

We have, once again, created a powerful constraining force that demands our attention, addictively. Too many humans now live in a virtual world in which their cell phone operates as a portal to a *faux* community that has the power to disrupt their well-being and keep them from getting what they really need: authentic relations with real people in real communities of support.

For those who know me, it easy to wonder why I am waxing so philosophically and evaluatively, given that I consider myself to be a hard social scientist who is supposed to be value-neutral. The answer is very simple. Most sociologists, at their core, have a heart and are concerned about what humans do to each other. What attracted me and so many others to sociology in our formative years was our dismay over social conditions, and our desire to somehow "do something" about them. Sociology was a natural major for college students in the United States because sociology was born in the USA with an emphasis on "social problems," just as it was in Europe with Auguste Comte's christening the new discipline with its Latin-Greek hybrid name: *sociology.*

For Comte, sociology was to be a hard science, but at the same time it was to be a science that could be used to remake societies by eliminating "pathologies," much as physicians seek to eliminate diseases. Of course, an immediate problem arises when sociology is seen in this dual role: (1) isolating the fundamental dynamics of the social universe and developing theoretical models and principles to understand these dynamics, on the science side, and (2) using this theoretical knowledge to address "social problems" and "social pathologies," on the applied science side. This problem is: Who decides what is a problem or pathology, on what basis do they make this judgment, and what gives them the right to do so?

How are we to know, for sure, what condition in society is normal or abnormal? For a social critic, an ideologue, a literary figure, a non-scientist, or a scientist in an undisciplined moment, this question is not a big problem, because certain conditions seem so "obviously" problematic. One just asserts that a condition is pathological with the intention of convincing others that such is indeed the case. But, for a scientist, we must have more "objective" criteria than just our own personal judgment, coupled with the *chutzpah* to make a pronouncement and clarion call for action. Sociologists have often been quite content to make such calls, and some even go so far as to see science "as part of the problem." Fortunately, many also assert that *science is the solution to the problems that plague humans in the present-day world.*

Creating Life Before Death is one such book. It is a book that goes back to some of the fundamental issues about the organization of societies that troubled early and mid-twentieth century sociologists like C. Wright Mills, Alvin W. Gouldner, and Robert Nisbet. In being "retro" in this sense, it is also a breath of fresh air in an environment that is now so strident and emotional, highly politicized, and yet rather gloomy. The "political correctness" that dominates so much of sociology, particularly in the United States, is no longer emancipating. Rather, it is yet another form of constraint and dogma within academia that has spread to the outside world.

Creating Life Before Death is somewhat of an antidote to gloomy academia, and thankfully avoids this current restriction on the sociological imagination by addressing the big issues: What are humans doing to themselves by creating social structures and cultures that dominate the individual and, in essence, go against the very nature of human beings? How can we become liberated from these sociocultural creations? This book offers a plan that sounds simple but is not so easily accomplished: Reduce the bureaucratization of social life and other restrictive conditions like crushing and enduring inequalities. Restore the individualism and a sense of an efficacious and self-directed self. And, most of all, reactivate not only our big brains but our big hearts to realize what it is to be human and, thereby, what it is to be humane.

As I have long argued for many years, humans are unique because of their emotionality as much as their big brains and capacities for speech and cultural production. Our big neocortex and capacities for rationality get too much of the attention for what is right, and often too much of the blame for what is wrong, with societies. Equally problematic is our emotionality, speech, and culture that blind us (even with our big brains) to what we have done to ourselves, and to virtually all life forms on earth. The group of scholars who have joined Bernard Phillips in developing *Creating Life Before Death* see the solution to problems in human societies as requiring not only (a) the development and then application of scientific knowledge made possible by our large neocortex, but also (b) the liberation of our emotions from the constraints imposed by modes of speech production and communication as well as by cultures. They sustain problematic social constructions and, thereby, damage each of us as human beings.

This project is an outgrowth of an earlier series of conferences among *The Sociological Imagination Group* that presented research papers during nine annual American Sociological Association meetings, starting at the turn of the century, and publishing them in three volumes. But this new book is more systematic and focused. It is a kind of public sociology, in Michael Burawoy's sense, but in a less obvious way. On the surface, it might seem quite "old school" in its heavy focus on bureaucracy, emotions, and the individual. But, in actual fact, it addresses the issues that were central to the founding generations of 19th Century sociologists, combined with the concerns of thinkers in the 20th Century after World War I.

All of these problems have gotten a bit lost in the last two decades. Concerns over discrimination against categories of persons by ethnicity, race, gender, and sexuality have come to dominate sociological discourse and research. These latter issues are also addressed by *Creating Life Before Death* because, in the end, this book is about liberating human beings from unnecessary constraints, and for creating new kinds of cultural and structural systems for organizing human societies. If there is to be a true public sociology, we cannot forget other discriminations, like those based upon social class, nor should we lose sight of what *Creating Life Before Death* seeks to rekindle: a concern for understanding the problems of modernity in general, and its effects on the well-being of persons in particular. It is a book that overlaps with some critical theories, like those by Jurgen Habermas and other 20th Century Marxists such as Max Horkheimer, Theodor Adorno, Antonio Gramsci and Erik Olin Wright. But it is not so dogmatic.

Creating Life Before Death does not fully answer the questions that I enumerated earlier about how we can objectively use science to decide what is problematic in society and among humans living in societies of the current modern era. Yet it rekindles what I was afraid was getting lost: concerns over the harmful effects of societies on the fundamental nature of humans. True, scholars as divergent as Jurgen Habermas, Thomas Scheff, Pierre Bourdieu and Anthony Giddens have carried the issues of the mid-20th Century into the 21st Century, especially the concern for the damage to humans' emotional well-being and efficacy of self in problematic social relations, engendered by restrictive social structures and cultural ideologies. *Creating Life Before Death* offers useful strategies for individuals to follow in their efforts to break the hold of sociocultural formations, to restore emotional balance, to revive self-reflection and self-efficacy, to reaffirm human individuality and dignity, and in so doing, to begin to remake societies.

In a book that I have just finished, *The Sociology of Human Nature*, I sought to isolate the evolved biological and neurological basis of human nature. My goal was to separate what is part of our inherited biology from the confounding effects of the sociocultural constructions in which we now live. I chose this topic because I wanted to look at what scholars have often only speculated about by using hard methods in biology that can allow for tracing behavioral capacities and propensities inherited from the ancestors of great apes and hominins, leading to humans who are still, at their biological core, evolved great apes.

I had not learned my motivation for pursuing this age-old topic in a new way until I read *Creating Life Before Death*. I was, perhaps subconsciously, trying to address the old issues that have long dominated intellectual discourse about the human condition. In order to conduct this discourse productively, we need to have a real understanding of what it means to be human in a biological sense. Nevertheless, I find a book like Christian Smiths' *What is a Person?* very useful and fascinating, even though it is somewhat speculative. I mention my book and highly recommend Smith's book not as a marketing ploy, but as other potentially useful efforts to address the problems highlighted in *Creating Life Before Death*.

In my new book, I view human nature as the evolved biology, honed by natural selection, to create the term *evolved complexes* revolving around (a) *the emotions complex*, (b) *the cognitive complex, (c) the interaction complex*, (d) *the psychology complex*, and (d) *the community complex*. These complexes, which constitute bundles of behavioral propensities and capacities that are hard-wired into the human brain, are all elaborations of behavioral capacities and propensities among humans' hominin ancestors. They evolved as natural selection reworked the biology and neurology of those ancestors by, first, expanding hominins' subcortical neurology generating emotions, and then, by growing the neocortex to hold large stores of stocks of knowledge and memories to be used in rapid decision making. And from these elaborations eventually came speech and cultural production.

After reading *Creating Life Before Death*, I was struck by how much the authors focused on many of the very elements in these complexes that I had isolated by using methods from biology and neurology to find humans' fundamental nature. This realization has given me much more confidence in *the validity of their analysis* as to what needs to be done for individuals and societies to bring the two into better compatibility. We need to re-make societies so that they are more compatible with the human nature that I have isolated in complexes or as the authors of *Creating Life Before Death* and Christian Smith in his *What is a Person?* have done. We must discover what it means to be human and thereby have a better sense for what humans need.

The first human societies of hunter-gatherers were highly compatible with humans' evolved nature. Later societies, including horticultural, pastoral, and agrarian ones, violated this nature. Industrial societies and later post-industrial societies began to reveal features that were potentially more compatible with this nature, but, sadly, went astray. Humans can never go back to their original Garden of Eden, as evident in simple hunting and gathering societies. But the authors of *Creating Life Before Death* have captured what needs to be done to make large and complex human societies of today more compatible with humans' nature as evolved great apes with dramatically expanded emotional and cognitive capacities that allowed for speech and culture.

From my perspective, we need to reclaim our biological inheritance—to begin to be guided, once again, by the fundamental nature of our humanity. And we must figure out ways to realize this nature much larger and more complex societies than those in which humans evolved. *Creating Life Before Death* offers an agenda and suggests various strategies for how humans can create and live in modern societies that are more in tune with human nature, although the authors do not quite phrase the matter in these terms. Reading the pages in this short volume is pleasant and easy, incorporating many insights from different traditions that have sought, at least implicitly, to understand human nature. This book is a very large step in the right direction for suggesting how it is possible to create less-constraining environments, and especially internal environments in which our sense of self lives in big, complex societies.

Jonathan H. Turner is the 38th University Professor of the University of California system. He received his BA degree from the University of California in 1965, and his MA in 1966 and PhD in 1968 from Cornell University. He is currently Director of the Institute for Theoretical Social Science, a small privately funded institute promoting what Turner, like Auguste Comte, prefers to call Social Physics. Previously he was Distinguished Professor of Sociology at the University of California, Riverside, and, more recently, Research Professor at the University of California, Santa Barbara.

Since his PhD in 1968, Turner has devoted his career to producing formal theories—systems of abstract principles and analytical models—of generic and universal properties and processes of the social universe. He has theorized at all levels of social reality, from the behavior and interaction of individuals through micro and meso structures to macro institutional, stratification, societal, and inter-societal systems. He considers key areas of more substantive specialization to include: sociology of emotions, social psychology more generally, ethnic relations, stratification, group dynamics, organizational ecology, institutional analysis, primatology, evolutionary sociology, neuro-sociology, evolutionary analysis in biology, and philosophy of science.

And, perhaps most relevant in the invitation for him to write a foreword to Creating Life Before Death, *he has always been committed to using sociology to address social problems. Indeed, he has been a strong advocate that, for want of a better name, he terms "social engineering," revolving around using theoretical principles and models to guide social policy and efforts to solve problems occurring at all levels of societal organization.*

His earlier work in this more applied area often revealed a clear evaluation of what is right, good, and just in societies and what is problematic, especially in American society. In more recent efforts over the last 25 years, he has tried to remain more value-neutral, to the degree that this is possible. He decided to do so in order to eliminate potential contamination from what he would like to see societies become, on the one hand, to a more value-neutral specification of what is possible (given the context in which sociology is used in applications), on the other hand. This position has made him somewhat controversial.

He remains, however, sympathetic to all efforts of sociologists to make the accumulated knowledge of the discipline available to the public at large and to clients in need of this knowledge. Again, not without controversy, he has advocated that there should be an engineering subfield and Ph.D. track in sociology, perhaps denoted by a less controversial name such as Sociological Practice.

He is the author or co-author of 43 books, 10 edited or co-edited books, and several hundred published research papers. His most recent book, The Sociology of Human Nature, *reflects his recent efforts over the last two decades to bring the analysis of biology and neurology into sociology. He is currently writing a book that refines his earlier theorizing on the dynamics of human social interaction, titled* The Sociology of Interpersonal Behavior.

Invitation to a Journey for Self-Discovery

Reader, have you ever wondered whether you were somehow missing out on life's possibilities?

Are there earlier dreams that you wish might have been fulfilled?

Will your lighting one little candle address deepening problems of society?

Do climate changes, racism, sexism, ageism, ethnocentrism, school shootings, and threats from nuclear, biological and chemical weapons of mass destruction make you feel there is little you can accomplish?

Have you lost the American dream of success through hard work, given the increasing gap between the rich and the poor?

Do you feel that you are an insignificant cog in the vast machine of society? Have you learned to go along in order to get along?

So it is that at this time in history, every single one of us is confronted by a double crisis.

The first crisis asks us: How can we hope to live a truly meaningful life before our deaths? Is it possible for us to experience a life full of understanding, joy and personal fulfillment?

The second crisis asks us: How can the human race possibly survive? Are we all doomed to an actual death delivered by threatening yet unsolved problems?

In the past, your authors have asked themselves these same questions and felt pessimism as the result of our answers.

However, we have emerged with optimism that knows no limits about the human potential. We have taken into account the full range of our personal experiences together with human achievements built on billions of years of biological evolution…

My name is Dr. Bernard Phillips. I hold a B.A. from Columbia University, a Master's Degree from Washington State University, and a Ph.D. from Cornell. I taught at the University of North Carolina, the University of Illinois, and Boston University, and co-founded the Section on Sociological Practice of the American Sociological Association.

I founded and directed "The Sociological Imagination Group," with annual meetings yielding three volumes that I edited. I've published four books on social research, two introductions to sociology, and other books, such as on terrorism and constructing the future. My essay, "Sociology's Next Steps?" was invited by *Contemporary Sociology* in 2019.

Most important, I have continued to be inspired by the interdisciplinary vision of C. Wright Mills, my mentor at Columbia. His book, *The Sociological Imagination,* was rated by members of the International Sociological Association as the second most influential book for sociologists published during the entire 20th century. Mills' work has encouraged me to put into practice a new vision for creating life before death...

Tom Savage's unique background combines 25 years as a minister and 23 years with the Sarasota, Florida, Sheriff's Department, where he retired as a lieutenant. He served churches in Belmont, Massachusetts, where he was ordained, and in Elgin, Illinois, Madison, Wisconsin, and Sarasota, Florida. Moving from pulpit to patrol car, the robe and badge provided experiences granted very few of us. They have yielded numerous stories found in this book.

Attempting to rise above the biased cultural contamination of one's own personal experiences in his native land, Mr. Savage has traveled to over eighty-nine countries, studying local traditions and beliefs. The goal he sought was an appreciation of unity within diversity, while championing individuality in community.

Tom Savage holds a B.A. from the University of Redlands, California, and a Master of Divinity and Master of Sacred Theology Degree from the Boston University School of Theology. He created a unique experiment in community policing with over ten thousand volunteers for a citizen patrol. He has served as the founder of the Sarasota Public Arts Fund. He serves on the Ringling College Scholarship Committee, and is a significant donor for philanthropic causes in the area...

The two of us working together, a scholar and a preacher, point toward reaching two diverse audiences: academics and the public in general. Books almost invariably focus on one group or the other. Those attempting to reach both often result in reaching neither.

However, we can succeed in our efforts if the general audience realizes the importance of academic credibility, and if the academic audience understands that a large readership is helped by stories. The joining of these two audiences can give our ideas the momentum they require to encourage widespread engagement toward a more meaningful life instead of an untimely death.

...

Andy Plotkin, my doctoral student at Boston University, started your authors on this quest seven years ago. His background, including immersion in the arts, an award for teaching, and a major production on television—not to also speak of his publications in sociology—has sharpened and broadened what readers see on these pages.

Neil Weiss, with his doctorate in business and teaching experience at Columbia, has deeply strengthened our wide-ranging approach. During our years of weekly conferences, Neil's deep commitment to enabling readers to apply our ideas has shaped this book.

Max Spitzer, by far the youngest author, was attracted to sociology by Andy Plotkin. Starting with C. Wright Mills, this results in four generations pointing in much the same direction. Max's own combined background in science, medicine and sociology succeeds in broadening still further our interdisciplinary orientation.

The result has been a work that parallels the diversity of the stories told by the twenty-four pilgrims in Geoffrey Chaucer's fourteenth-century *Canterbury Tales* who were on their way to visit the shrine of Saint Thomas Becket. Our own tale gathers together over two hundred voices. Your authors are on a journey to address the twin problems of personal meaninglessness and increasing worldwide problems. This is a journey that we invite readers to share, adding their voices to those in this book.

...

Our vision is based on the incredible potential, largely unfulfilled, of every single human being who walks the planet. We have integrated the two most powerful tools that humans have created: language and the scientific method. They can be placed in the hands of each one of us!

Addressing our double crisis, people have failed to understand that a direction for resolving the first one, achieving a meaningful life, can yield a solution for the second one, solving our escalating problems. It is the further development of the individual that is the basis for the continued evolution of society. Attention must be paid to the individual's awesome possibilities for continuing to grow intellectually, emotionally, and in problem-solving abilities throughout life.

Each one of us, and not just professional scientists, has the possibility of learning to make use of the full power of the scientific method.

Each one of us, and not just English professors, can learn to fully harness the enormous powers of language.

Working toward one's continuing personal evolution is not a selfish procedure, given that it will also point toward the solution of society's problems.

We are not calling for "see-saw" behavior, where one learns to put down others or oneself, but rather "stairway" behavior, where we help one another continue to climb.

Erich Fromm, the renowned psychoanalyst and author, claimed: "The failure of modern culture...lies not in the fact that people...are too selfish, but that they do not love themselves" (1947/1976: 139).

What, then, stands in the way of personal and societal continuing development or evolution?

...

Tom Savage has a story producing insight into the nature of our problems as well as a direction for solving them. It took place when he was seven years old and had to do with his first crisis of faith. A volunteer Sunday school teacher had just told his class the story of the Israelites' escape from Egypt. At the Red Sea, Moses had parted the waters, and the Jews all went safely through. But when Pharaoh with his army and chariots followed in hot pursuit, Moses closed the waters over them.

At that point, Tom jumped up and yelled, "What happened to the horses? Surely God didn't drown the horses!" The poor teacher, sputtering, could offer no defense. Tom would not calm down, for he believed in an all-powerful and all-righteous God, and he would not tolerate a teacher who dared to stray from those beliefs. The result, however, was that Tom became perhaps the first kid ever to be kicked out of Sunday school.

Tom had uncovered three key components of our bureaucratic way of life: Patterns of (1) persisting hierarchy, (2) personal conformity to the powers that be, and (3) narrow specialization without integrating knowledge.

What Tom also achieved with his outburst was nothing less than illustrating how to confront effectively that way of life: He dared to (1) question authority, (2) develop his own understanding, and (3) move beyond the simplicity or narrowness of the ideas of authorities, as illustrated by the good-evil biblical story.

A bureaucracy is an organization with a division of labor that is governed by leaders who lay down explicit rules. Tom's church illustrated this pattern of behavior. It was governed by denominational leaders, a council of elders, a pastor, voluntary teachers, and written and unwritten rules to be followed. Its division of labor is indicated by the different duties of these individuals, all of whom followed church rules.

Just as Tom questioned the ideas of his teacher, so we question a way of life that is yielding unsolved and highly threatening problems, such as aggression of all kinds, addiction, climate change, and a failure to teach individuals how to develop their full potential.

Just as Tom refused to conform to the authority of his teacher by standing up to shout his views, so we challenge existing authorities whom we see as fiddling while Rome is burning.

Just as this seven-year-old saw the limitations of scripture, so we call out the ignorance resulting from narrow specialization with limited integration of knowledge of human behavior and human problems.

...

To understand the nature of bureaucracy more concretely, here is a story that Tom Savage experienced while he was a minister. An elderly widow had a pie-plate collection of great beauty and high monetary value. She would bring desserts on them to church suppers, and she was immensely proud of herself for doing so. However, members of the congregation were worried that the plates might get chipped or broken, although they certainly appreciated the use of them.

Their worst fears were realized when one of the plates turned out to be missing. The widow immediately left the church with this letter of resignation: "To the church board: I can no longer entrust the salvation of my immortal soul to an institution that cannot keep watch over a mere pie-plate."

Yet that action completely followed from the situation she had set up in the first place when she volunteered her tableware collection. She saw use of those plates as far superior to what the others in the congregation were able to offer. Her view of the importance of those plates over everything else revealed a very narrow understanding. Her resignation from the church illustrated behavior that conformed to her beliefs about her own superiority. She failed to take into account the many benefits and wide range of experiences she had had as a long-standing member of the congregation.

...

Before we proceed, let us play devil's advocate and question whether bureaucracy—with its focus on hierarchy, conformity and lack of breadth—is, in fact, our central problem.

Perhaps it is the nature of our economy that is most problematic. Our need for secure employment with livable wages leads us to abandon our personal priorities in favor of the requirements of our authorities. We know that the gap between the rich and the poor has been growing rapidly over the last decades, with the super-wealthy one percent of the population gaining the greatest rewards, and with the rest of us making do with the remainder.

Medical care costs continue to skyrocket, as do costs of college tuition. How does a family, with an ordinary income and little access to affordable health insurance, survive when a catastrophic illness occurs? How can they possibly afford to send their children to college on the assumption that they are not superstars who can earn scholarships?

How can students start a family and buy a home when they are enslaved by a lifetime of debt?

How can people with limited income afford to retire in their sixties, given wage stagnation that has been continuing over the decades?

What could be more basic than the problem of safety for parents and their children living in inner cities, yet gang warfare on their streets keeps them prisoners in their homes.

There is also the world's inability to control devastating hurricanes, wildfires and other climate-related catastrophes.

Problems of suicide and drug-related deaths have produced an opioid crisis.

Unsolved problems of bullying, and the abuse of women at home and in the workplace, display the failures of society.

How can we expect our schoolchildren to endure continuing mass-shootings, with no effective procedures for eliminating this violence?

If so much of our resources continues to feed what President Eisenhower called "the military-industrial complex," then little will remain to provide a livable standard of living for the rest of us.

The cowardice of political leaders is a continuing problem. Rather than focusing on significant issues, a great many of them are concerned only with their own re-election. Many have become puppets of special interest groups who shower them with money for their re-election campaigns. Instead of serving their constituents, far too many do not feel free to move away from conformity to party bosses.

These issues are all quite visible, for we hear about and see them through the mass media. By contrast, bureaucracy is invisible.

Since almost all social science concepts, such as "bureaucracy," invoke invisible phenomena, how can we learn to understand the nature of our problems so that we can confront them? This is exactly what we are asking readers to do: learn to use concepts to make visible what is presently invisible.

We might see bureaucracy as the invisible disease, while the above visible problems are the symptoms of the disease. Fighting one of the symptoms will not cure the broad disease, granting that it might be helpful. Fighting the disease requires, by contrast, a much wider approach that affects all of the symptoms.

...

Ann Landers received a letter from a reader who wrote: "It wasn't the senior citizens who took melody out of music, beauty out of art, pride out of appearance, romance out of love, commitment out of marriage, responsibility out of parenthood, togetherness out of family, learning out of education, loyalty out of Americanism, service out of patriotism, hearth out of home, civility out of behavior, refinement out of language, dedication out of employment, prudence out of spending, the loss of patience and tolerance in relationships."

What could have been added to that letter, however, is an understanding that all of these changes are symptoms of a disease that remains largely invisible. That disease is a way of life with its emphasis on patterns of conformity to people in charge of us, coupled with blinders that keep us focused on narrow paths.

...

Such paths are illustrated by a Taoist story. A group of blind men hear of a strange animal, called an elephant, which has been brought into their town. They are curious about the nature of this animal, and so they begin to look for it. When they finally find an elephant, they all use their hands to grope about it.

One of them, whose hands land on the trunk, says, "This being is like a thick snake." Another, who touches the elephant's ear, claims that the animal is like a fan. As for another, who touches its leg, argues that the elephant is like a tree-trunk. The blind man who places his hand on the elephant's side, says, "The elephant is a wall." Yet another who feels its tail describes the elephant as a rope. The last one feels its tusk and states, "The animal is like a spear."

Each of the six blind men was completely correct on the basis of what he experienced, yet none of their conclusions came close to describing what an elephant really looks like. This is much the same as what specialized social scientists have discovered, given their failure to integrate their knowledge. The result of their failure is a matter of life and death for the rest of us. For if such investigations fail to help us understand the nature of our highly threatening and increasing problems, then those problems will do us in.

Recall the 9/11 disaster at the World Trade Center and Pentagon. Specialized knowledge about the potential for that catastrophe was learned by the CIA, FBI, State Department and NSA. Yet there was no sharing among those organizations, which had developed patterns of isolation from one another.

We had the explosion of the space shuttle Challenger due to an O-ring failure. In all likelihood, the O-ring would have been fixed if employees in different departments had pooled their knowledge with one another. Also, employees might well have notified management of the O-ring problem if hierarchical relationships had not severely limited such communication.

In the academic world, Isaac Newton expressed the importance of integrating knowledge when he wrote, "If I have seen further it is by standing on the shoulders of giants." The number of sections of the American Sociological Association was only six when I started teaching, yet it now stands at fifty-two, and counting, with very little communication across the various sections.

A similar focus on narrow specialization without the integration of knowledge pervades the other social sciences as well. Given the complexity of human behavior, that lack of communication violates the central scientific requirement that one must build on the full range of relevant information.

…

Can you believe that the failure to integrate knowledge by those in charge of nuclear warfare in the U.S. and Russia has resulted in eleven documented near-catastrophes between 1956 and 2010? On each occasion, the world almost stumbled into a nuclear missile exchange because of misinterpreted warning signals.

Except for extremely fortunate circumstances, you might not have survived to read these words, and I might not have survived to write them.

To illustrate just one of these near-disasters for the human race, on September 26, 1983, a satellite early-warning system near Moscow reported the launch of one American Minuteman ICBM. Soon after, it reported that five missiles had been launched.

Convinced that a real American offensive would involve many more missiles, Lieutenant Colonel Stanislav Petrov of the Soviet Air Defense Forces refused to acknowledge the threat as legitimate, and convinced his superiors that it was a false alarm until this could be confirmed by ground radar. But what if Petrov had conformed to the wishes of his superiors?

If American leaders had noted this false alarm and had come to believe that it was an excuse for the Soviet Union to launch missiles at America, then the U.S. might well have launched missiles at the Soviet Union in response.

Such accidental dangers are not merely occurrences that happened in the past and can no longer occur. As reported in *The New York Times* on January 13, 2018, this emergency alert was sent out to all available cellphones across Hawaii: "**Emergency Alert** BALLISTIC MISSILE THREAT INBOUND TO HAWAII. SEEK IMMEDIATE SHELTER. THIS IS NOT A DRILL."

Hawaii had been on high alert since December 2017, staging monthly air-raid drills complete with sirens, as a result of the escalating nuclear threats exchanged by North Korea's Kim Jong-un and Donald Trump. A missile from North Korea would take no more than 30 minutes to reach Hawaii.

Can you imagine the panic throughout the state that this caused? There were pictures on television of people everywhere running for their lives. Paul Wilson, a professor at Brigham Young University-Hawaii, said on Twitter, ". . . this was the most terrifying few minutes of my LIFE."

Matt LoPresti, a state representative, told CNN that he and his family headed for a bathroom. "I was sitting in the bathtub with my children, saying our prayers," he said. Natalie Haena, 38, of Honolulu, stated, "There's nothing to prep for a missile coming in. We have no bomb shelters or anything like that. There's nowhere to go." Allyson Niven, who lives in Kailua-Kona, felt she was experiencing her final minutes alive. "We fully felt like we were about to die," she said.

This accident could have resulted in far more than panic throughout Hawaii. North Korea could have interpreted this false alarm as an excuse to launch missiles toward the U.S.

As it happened, during a Hawaii Emergency Management Agency "are-you-ready" drill, an employee mistakenly pushed the button on a computer that actually sent out the alert throughout the state, rather than the button that was simply testing the system. When asked by the system if he was sure he wanted to send the message, he answered "yes." It then took a full 38 minutes to issue this statement: "There is no missile threat or danger to the State of Hawaii. Repeat. False Alarm."

Chris Tacker, a veteran who lives in Kealakekua, said, "I didn't know where to go. Anyone try to dig a hole in lava? Good luck trying to build a shelter. I'm stocking my liquor cabinet." Still, she added, "If we don't have our sense of humor about this, it's all over."

...

Let us never forget the actual catastrophe of the Holocaust, which has been the greatest single challenge to the morality of our way of life. For Germany was a culturally advanced nation with a democratically elected government. How could that unbelievable human tragedy actually have occurred? The philosopher Hannah Arendt had been asked by *The New Yorker* magazine to cover the trial of one of Hitler's key officials involved in the Holocaust, with its slaughter of six million Jews and millions of others.

Her conclusions appeared in *Eichmann in Jerusalem: A Report on the Banality of Evil* (1963/1977). For her, the trial of Adolph Eichmann demonstrated that we must never forget the central role of bureaucracy in the slaughter of innocents, for it is the existence of bureaucracy that is a central problem of society. She viewed Eichmann as deserving punishment for his enormous crimes against humanity. But behind Eichmann's actions was the bureaucratic organization of Nazi Germany.

Yet Arendt's profound insight into the causes of the Holocaust has fallen on deaf ears. For example, a recent film about Adolph Eichmann, *Operation Finale*, avoids any treatment of the role of bureaucracy in its focus on Eichmann's guilt.

Yes, the world seems full of a multitude of problems without solutions. Tom Savage shares with us his memory of officiating at what he called "the wedding from hell."

It isn't just bureaucracy that allows individuals to fail to assume personal responsibility for their behavior. In a world filled with chance and change, the supposed best plans of mice and men, too, can end up in chaos. The unfortunate, unexpected, unanticipated events in life also play a role in potential mishaps.

"In terms of numbers in the wedding party, it was the largest I had ever worked with. Bride, groom, groom's men, bridesmaids, ushers, flower girls, ring bearer, over twenty-two in all, standing before me in a church filled with over one-thousand guests. It was a beautiful sight to behold. Everyone, after a disastrous wedding rehearsal, had managed to end up in the right place on the wedding day. It was truly a beautiful sight to behold.

"I opened my book and began the service. 'Dearly beloved, we are gathered together' . . . CRASH. The first bridesmaid had collapsed to the floor in a pile of chiffon. Two groom's men rushed over, picked her up, and placed her in a front pew. I began again, 'Dearly beloved'...CRASH. A second bridesmaid fell over, but this one fell forward into a flowered rope connected to a nine-candle candelabrum and half the decorations on the right side of the church. Now, in addition to picking the girl up, the ushers were doing a Mexican Hat Dance to stamp out the candles before the whole place went up in flames.

"At the same time, a nervous groom began hyper-ventilating, gasping for air. The bride began to cry, and at this point I stopped the service, taking all participants off into a nearby room, trying to figure out what in the hell was happening. I soon learned that the bridesmaids had all decided not to eat anything for two days before the wedding to appear extra thin. And this, plus being pumped up with nervous adrenalin, caused the fainting.

"At that point the bride announced she wanted to start the whole ceremony all over from the beginning. Once again, down the aisle she came on the arm of her father when, suddenly, she whirled around and raced out of the sanctuary. The congregation gasped! Had she changed her mind? No! But she did have to change her pants, having exploded with diarrhea in her wedding dress.

"An hour later, it all ended well. I skipped the reception, but blessed the union with a drink at home. Amen!"

In a July 2019 featured essay—"Sociology's Next Steps?"—invited by *Contemporary Sociology*, the journal of reviews for that discipline, I quoted an ancient Japanese proverb: "A vision without action is a daydream. But action without a vision is a nightmare."

As a sociologist, my vision or goal built on the theories of the German sociologist, Jurgen Habermas (1981), in calling for people's "personal emancipation" from our patterns of conforming to persisting hierarchy. I equally depended on the theories of the British sociologist, Anthony Giddens (1984), who emphasized the importance of persisting social behavior or social structures with his concept of "structuration."

Those ideas suggested my alternative to our present way of life:

> Alternatively, suppose that we could learn to move away from conformity to society's patterns of social stratification [persisting hierarchy] by educating the individual to achieve a series of self-images with ever greater ability to make progress on personal and world problems, based on one's actual achievement of such abilities.

> In that way we would be extending Giddens' idea of structuration to include the continuing development of the individual, for self-image is indeed a structure, a personality structure. And also in that way we would be achieving what Habermas called personal emancipation.

> This would call for a vision of continuing personal development extending far beyond the achievements of those at the pinnacles of our stratified social structures.

> Such a vision would recapture the optimism of the Enlightenment and the utopian era of the 19th Century. Among social scientists, it would call for a new focus on the individual without excluding attention to social structures. (2019: 384)

As for action, I followed Carl G. Jung in his call for making conscious what was previously unconscious, or making visible what was previously invisible, in his *The Undiscovered Self* (1957/2006). I also joined contemporary thinkers who have emphasized "public sociology," where they present their findings in the mass media (for example: Burawoy (2008a, 2008b), Badgett (2016), Stein and Daniels, (2017), and Sternheimer (2017).

I ended my essay by calling on sociologists to follow their ideas with actions, based on an understanding of their own powers and the present needs of society.

This goal or value of continuing personal development or evolution has been hinted at throughout history by many individuals. Socrates claimed that "the unexamined life is not worth living." St. Luke's advice in the New Testament is, "Physician, heal thyself." Voltaire, the French philosopher of the Enlightenment era, stated, "We must cultivate our garden." Funakoshi, the father of modern karate, claimed: "First know yourself, then know others." Walt Kelly's cartoon character, the opossum Pogo, exclaimed when he saw litter under a tree, "We have met the enemy and he is us."

As for how we might define "personal evolution," we can turn to the film, *The Wizard of Oz*, for some insight.

When the Scarecrow asks the Wizard for a brain, he responds: "Back where I come from we have universities, seats of great learning—where men go to becomegreat thinkers, and when they come out, they think deep thoughts—and with no more brains than you have. "

Replying to the Tin Man, the Wizard tells him: "Back where I come from there are men who do nothing all day but good deeds. And their hearts are no bigger than yours."

To the Lion, he says: "Back where I come from, we have men who are called heroes. Once a year, they take their fortitude out of mothballs and parade it down the main street of the city. And they have no more courage than you have. "

It is the Wizard's focus on the basic equality of every single human being—regardless of race, gender, ethnic or religious background, nationality, age, or sexual orientation—that is the hallmark of democracy. Can we even imagine how we and the world would change if more of us came to believe the Wizard's truths for ourselves? We would see ourselves as no less than anyone else, including the movers and shakers of the world.

...

Yet this book's message takes a step beyond the advice of the Wizard. We envision the potential of all individuals for continuing personal improvement or development in all aspects of life, with no limit as to how far we can go. More specifically, we might define "personal evolution" as the individual's increasing intellectual and emotional ability to solve problems. Following *The Wizard of Oz*, this gets at one's "head," "heart" and "hand."

We see this three-fold orientation to human development in the work of Jane Addams, the philosopher who founded the discipline of social work. She wrote these words in her *Democracy and Social Ethics* (1902): "A conception of Democracy not merely as a sentiment which desires the well-being of all men ["**heart**"], nor yet as a creed which believes in the essential dignity and equality of all men ["**head**"], but as that which affords a rule of living as well as a test of faith ["**hand**"]" (boldface added, quoted in Knowles, 2004: 3,18).

It is intellect that can create an image of one's own continuing improvement, emotions that yield the motivation to move toward that goal, and action that actually carries one toward fulfilling that vision.

John Dewey, in his *Reconstruction in Philosophy* (1920/1948) carried forward Addams' vision. He wrote: "Democracy has many meanings, but if it has a moral meaning, it is found in resolving that the supreme test of all political institutions and industrial arrangements shall be the contribution they make to the all-around growth of every member of society" (186). He envisioned that the central mission of government, business, education, religion, and the family should be to "educate every individual into the full stature of his possibility" (186).

...

Granting that our vision of personal evolution is a most democratic idea, where is the evidence for this supposed potential that we all have? Is this no more than a pipe dream, an ideal that is very far from reality? Is it actually the case that we are all severely limited in many ways, such as in our intelligence or capacity to learn?

Contemporary research has given the lie to the idea that our intelligence is fixed. This false idea, however, meshes so well with our emphasis on winners and losers in the economy, in schools, in sports, in games, and everywhere else.

The result is absolutely disastrous for all of us, including those who have done well on this supposed measure of our potential to gain understanding. We learn to limit our aspirations as a result, failing to take the advice of the English poet, Robert Browning: "Ah, but a man's reach should exceed his grasp, Or what's a heaven for?"

David Shenk's *The Genius in All of Us: Why Everything You've Been Told About Genetics, Talent, and IQ is Wrong* (2010) is only one of many new studies that successfully challenge our dated ideas that we humans are limited by our IQ. For evidence, he cites studies demonstrating that our genes are influenced by their interaction with all kinds of environmental stimuli.

Richard E. Nisbett, a psychology professor at the University of Michigan, systematically documents the idea that IQ can be changed by environmental factors in his *Intelligence and How to Get It: Why Schools and Culture Count* (2009).

To illustrate how IQ can be changed, experimental psychologists had students in an elementary school take a series of little-known IQ tests. They then gave their teachers lists of students who supposedly were "spurters" or "late bloomers," when in fact those students were chosen by a table of random numbers.

After a one-year period, the result was substantial increases in IQ on well-known intelligence tests among supposed late bloomers, by contrast with the other students. It was concluded that those increases in IQ resulted from their teachers' expectations (Rosenthal and Jacobsen, 1968).

Granting that we are not limited by IQ, these studies indicate the human capacity to continue to learn throughout life. The noted biologist Stephen Jay Gould stated as much in his *The Mismeasure of Man:*

> We are, in a more than metaphorical sense, permanent children...Many central features of our anatomy link us with fetal and juvenile stages of primates: small face, vaulted cranium and large brain in relation to body size, unrotated big toe, foramen magnum under the skull for correct orientation of the head in upright posture, primary distribution of hair on head, armpits and pubic areas...
>
> In other mammals, exploration, play, and flexibility of behavior are qualities of juveniles, only rarely of adults. We retain not only the anatomical stamp of childhood, but its mental flexibility...Humans are learning animals. (Gould, 1981: 333-334)

If our biological nature indicates that we can continue to learn throughout our lives, then we can learn to develop emotionally as well as in our ability to solve problems, and not just intellectually. In other words, we can continue to move toward fulfilling the full range of our capacities.

We have an example of such personal evolution from the rapid reconstruction of German and Japanese industry following World War II, financed by America's Marshall Plan. Focusing in particular on Japan, what developed throughout their companies was a culture of continuous improvement, where all employees no less than management were actively involved.

They developed the idea of "*kaizen*" or "continuous improvement." The idea of *kaizen* was accompanied by both emotional commitment to this idea as well as actual improvement. This approach was by no means limited to long-term projects. An improvement could take place within a few hours or a day. *Kaizen* includes both the reorganization of an entire area of production as well as the improvement by an individual of his or her own work.

Crucial to the achievement of *kaizen* was the use of the scientific method by workers and administrators, and not just by professional scientists. A central figure in helping the Japanese make use of that method throughout the workday was William Edwards Deming, an American engineer, statistician, professor, author, lecturer, and management consultant with a background in mathematical physics.

As a result, Japanese products experienced a metamorphosis from cheap throwaways to extremely high quality, as illustrated by the worldwide purchases of Toyota cars. The Emperor of Japan awarded Deming the Order of the Sacred Treasure in 1960, and an annual Deming Prize was set up. In the U.S., President Ronald Reagan honored him with the National Medal of Technology, and the National Academy of Sciences presented him with the Distinguished Career in Science award.

How are we to understand more fully just how Deming and others, working with Japanese manufacturers, were able to proceed with their incredible achievements? How was it possible for ordinary workers to take on the *kaizen* idea of continuing improvement?

In the French dramatist Moliere's play, *Le Bourgeois Gentilhomme*, Monsieur Jourdain learns from his philosophy teacher that he is speaking prose. He remarks: "Good heavens! For more than forty years I have been speaking prose without knowing it."

In the same way, we all have been using to an extent language's enormous abilities to solve our problems in everyday life without knowing much about the nature of those extraordinary powers. For it is our complex languages that sharply differentiate us humans for all other organisms throughout the known universe. And every single one of us has also been using to some degree the scientific method in everyday life without realizing it. That method has been powerful enough to have shaped the world over the past five centuries.

The psychologist George A. Kelly helps us to understand just how this has been happening in his *A Theory of Personality*. He writes not just about professional scientists with all of their degrees, their publications, and their honors, but about all of us:

To a large degree...the blueprint of human progress has been given the label of "science." Let us then...have a look at man-the-scientist...Might not the individual man...assume more of the stature of a scientist, ever seeking to predict and control the course of events with which he is involved? Would he not have his theories, test his hypotheses, and weight his experimental evidence? (1963: 4)

Victor Borge, the comic pianist, tells the story of a relative who was an amateur scientist. He first tried to cross a sponge with an Idaho potato. It tasted awful, but it sure as hell held a lot of gravy. Moving on, he tried to develop a formula for a new drink sensation that he called "Four-up." It failed, so he tried "Five-up" and "Six-up," with no success. So he gave up. Little did he know how close he came.

...

The key steps of the scientific method, which is a problem-solving procedure that builds on language and includes a wide range of our abilities, are:

(1) Gaining awareness of a problem, developing ideas or hypotheses about what causes the problem, and developing ideas about how to solve the problem.

(2) Becoming emotionally committed to achieving a solution.

(3) Acting to make progress on the problem, or to solve it.

(4) Repeating steps 1, 2 and 3 as often as necessary to continue to make progress on, or solve, the problem.

We can make use of a "pendulum metaphor" for the scientific method to help us understand its nature, illustrating the importance of language. Following the nature of metaphors, the pendulum metaphor uses a concrete experience—our image of a swinging pendulum—to help us understand something that is abstract or invisible, which is in this case the scientific method.

Let us imagine a pendulum swinging in ever-widening arcs. Each swing to the left can represent further understanding of how to solve a problem, and emotional commitment to doing so. Each swing to the right can stand for further progress toward actually solving it. The first two steps of the scientific method correspond to a swing to the left; the third step can be linked to a swing to the right; and the fourth step repeats these swings back and forth.

Here, then, is a direction for achieving increasing productivity throughout the world of economic activity by applying the *kaizen* idea ever more widely. This can yield over time the resources for yielding an ever more egalitarian society. When applied to political and not just economic organizations, it can result in an increasing ability to solve political problems throughout the world.

Yet how can the *kaizen* idea be extended from the workplace to the everyday lives of workers, managers and owners? The following pages can enable us to answer this question. Our optimism is based on the idea that we are all, biologically, learning animals, and there is no limit to how much we can learn. We can:

Learn to make visible our bureaucratic way of life that has remained invisible—or become conscious of what has remained unconscious—yielding motivation to change that way of life.

Learn to love ourselves no less than others, following Erich Fromm.

Learn to question authority, just as Tom did when he was seven years old.

Learn to focus on the incredible potentials of the individual, just as I indicated in my *Contemporary Sociology* essay.

Learn not to worship the rich, the famous and the powerful, just as the Wizard of Oz advised.

Learn to see democracy not just as a creed, but also as a sentiment and a rule of living, following Jane Addams' vision.

Learn to see one's IQ as a partial measure of ability, but certainly not as a measure of one's capacity to learn.

Learn to understand that one is already employing the most powerful tools that we humans have created: language and the scientific method.

Learn not to blame oneself for one's failures, but to recognize the power of invisible forces that are involved.

Learn not to blame others for their aggressive behavior, for they are victims of those same forces.

Learn to develop a vision of one's continuing improvement throughout one's everyday life.

Our capacity to learn about anything and everything illustrates a culmination of the interactive nature of the universe. The Big Bang some fourteen billion years ago produced a universe where no part of the world can be completely isolated from any other part.

As that interaction proceeded, it yielded the molecules that proved to become the basis for the origin of minute living things. Over billions of years this continuing process yielded organisms with ever greater ability to   interact with their environment and, as a result, solve their problems of existence and reproduction.

We humans finally appeared on the scene quite recently. Our inventions of language and the scientific method have given us the capacity—through continual learning—to solve problems that are ever more difficult and far-reaching than simply existence and reproduction.

Our educational institutions—formal and informal—have failed to teach us more than the very beginnings of the nature of our incredible capacities and how to transform them into abilities. Instead, we have remained victims of a bureaucratic way of life that has taught even Einstein, Shakespeare and Madam Curie of their drastic intellectual, emotional, and problem-solving limitations. Those deficiencies have in turn yielded ever more threatening problems to our very existence.

As we come to understand just who we are and what we are capable of accomplishing, we will come to see ourselves as standing at the very pinnacle of what the universe has yielded. It is that self-perception, in turn, which can enable us all to travel the yellow brick road of continuing personal and world development. It is an exceedingly democratic road, for each of us can work on our own unique tasks. We can scarcely imagine what lies over the rainbow.

A story Tom told me that illustrates our focus on the overriding importance of the individual has to do with his experiences as a minister for a church in Elgin, Illinois. A representative of a nearby funeral home asked him to provide a memorial service for an individual whose family had no church connections. He received a few notes about the deceased just before the service, allowing him to insert the person's name into his generalizations about the meaning and significance of human life.

Standing at the lectern, the closed coffin before him, an usher came running up and handed him a note, which read, "It isn't Mrs. Johnson," the name on all his information sheets. No other information indicated just who was in the coffin. This was the only funeral service he ever performed where he wasn't even able to use any pronouns. "What's in a name?" he thought. "Everything!" From his own perspective, the centrality of a name suggests the incredible potential of every single one of us.

Many of us recognize this nursery rhyme riddle: "As I was going to St. Ives, I met a man with seven wives. Every wife had seven sacks, every sack had seven cats, every cat had seven kitts. Kitts, cats, sacks, wives, how many were going to St. Ives?"

How many of us became confused, counting, multiplying bags, cats and kitts, coming up with a wrong answer, forgetting to add the man himself, and still being incorrect? Pay no attention to the man "coming from" St. Ives, burdened with his menagerie of wives, sacks, cats, and kitts, who has lost his way and any sense of purpose.

The answer is at the beginning: "As I was going to St. Ives..." The answer is "one." It is *you* who are going on a journey. Your purpose is illustrated by your reading this book.

> It is *you* who will learn to travel the path of renewed self-discovery. It is *you* who will learn to fulfill your birthright as a human being.

It is *you* who will learn to experience a self-confidence you've never felt before.

It is *you* who will use this book as a guide to a wonderful life before death.

Our most powerful tools, language and the scientific method, will guide us throughout the six chapters to follow. Parts One, Two and Three emphasize the steps of the scientific method that can lead us away from conformity and aggression. No longer should we see those tools as the province of English professors and physicists. They are procedures we've already been using throughout our lives, just as Monsieur Jourdain was speaking prose all his life.

This is what readers and authors will accomplish, based on the combination of our powers and the present needs of society.

Let us now proceed to learn, one step at a time, to release these powers.

Part 1

Vision: ("Head")

CHAPTER 1

The Problem: Our Failed Bureaucratic Vision

In Arthur Miller's play, *Death of a Salesman*, we see the failure of a life. We feel the impact of that tragedy for all individuals.

Willy Loman believed in the American dream of financial success through hard work. He idolizes his older brother, a diamond tycoon, who said: "When I was seventeen I walked into the jungle, and when I was 21, I walked out. And by God I was rich." Yet Willy has never been able to achieve economic success. He tried to teach his sons, Biff and Harold, his own mantra, yet their failures replay Willy's.

It is Willy's habitual narrow approach to life that has become his greatest enemy. This prevented him from being happy with what he already had. His resulting failure cost him both family and friends, plus any sense of joy in his work.

Our habits are so taken for granted that they remain basically invisible to us. This has become a chief problem in our lives. Willy has just conformed to this reality.

Emerson reminds us, "Whoso would be a man must be a nonconformist." Here, conformity equals mediocrity.

Willy's despair increases when his son, Biff, finds him in a hotel room with a woman who wasn't his mother. Adding to Willy's anguish, he is fired from his job.

Desperate, Willy develops a scheme to kill himself in order to give Biff his insurance money. Now, in his unhinged mind, his long-dead older brother appears and approves of his idea. The play ends with a funeral scene.

We end up with a half-broken heart as well.

Let's face it. To a large extent, we are all Willy Loman. For we, too, have been shaped by the false idea that winning and money are everything. Granted, most of us are not planning to commit suicide because of our failures. Still, many continue to lead lives that are in fact killing them without realizing that they can turn their lives around.

...

It is of overwhelming importance for societies to develop a broad and long-term image of the future that promises to solve the basic problems confronting all of us. Those problems include not just those that challenged Willy Loman, but others as well.

For example, on January 24, 2019, the *Bulletin of the Atomic Scientists*—with their Board of Sponsors including 15 Nobel laureates—set their Doomsday clock at 2 minutes to Midnight. Huge nuclear and climate-change issues have placed the "future of civilization in extraordinary danger."

It is a vision that is the very first step of the scientific method. Does one have a vision of continuing improvement, following the *kaizen* direction? Or does one's vision conform to the pessimism in such apocalyptic films as *On the Beach*, depicting the end of the human race as the result of World War III?

"In the country of the blind the one-eyed man is king," wrote Erasmus, the Dutch humanist, five hundred years ago. Apparently, we do live in the country of the blind. Just as the ideas of social scientists are invisible, we remain unable to open our eyes to a world of endless possibilities for all of us.

Where is an optimistic vision of progress for the individual and society? Who among our leaders has given us a direction, not merely for confronting today's problems, but for solving the world's problems, and then going on from there? What about an image for the individual to move away from repetitive tasks so as to fulfill dreams of an exciting and meaningful life, with no limits to personal development?

Where is the educator, the governmental official, the business CEO, the religious leader, the military man, who has developed such long-term goals? They are all AOL, absent without leave.

President George H. W. Bush's response to the suggestion that he turn his attention from short-term campaign objectives to long-term goals was: "Oh, the vision thing." By contrast with short-term goals, he had not thought about developing long-term images of the future.

President Bush is not alone. He is joined by almost all other political leaders. As a result, we have little promise for tackling the big problems of societies throughout the world. Neither is there much promise for helping individuals develop truly meaningful personal lives.

The image of a see-saw or teeter-totter can help us to understand two central parts of a vision of the future, which form the two sections of this chapter. The first is the idea that this recreational object is tied down to the ground, limiting the height that one can move up. This concrete or visible situation can serve as a metaphor, or stand for an abstract idea. We name that abstract idea "Conformity to Our Present Way of Life," the heading for the first part of this chapter.

When we move up on the see-saw, we push someone else down, metaphorically suggesting a pattern of aggression, as illustrated by war, terrorism, racism and bullying. Also, when we push ourselves down we might see this as a metaphor for aggression against oneself, as illustrated by patterns of addiction, lack of self-confidence, and even suicide. We label such behavior, our heading for the second part of this chapter, "Frustration and Aggression."

CONFORMITY TO OUR PRESENT WAY OF LIFE

Given the importance of integrating knowledge in order to make visible the invisible forces operating on us, we must turn to early figures in the history of the social sciences who preceded the present-day emphasis on narrow specialization with minimal linking of knowledge.

One such figure was Max Weber, a founder of the discipline of sociology with his work at the beginning of the 20th Century. He was a German sociologist, philosopher, jurist and political economist who is known to this day as having given us our basic understanding of the nature of bureaucracy (1922/2013). Weber saw the advantages of contemporary bureaucratic organizations over pre-industrial bureaucracies, given the education of modern administrators and workers. Yet he saw no alternative patterns of organization that were better.

Weber also gave us a powerful image in his *The Protestant Ethic and the Spirit of Capitalism* (1958). He saw capitalism as motivating people to work hard and become wealthy, yet leading them as a result to dwell in the "iron cage" of bureaucracy. Thus, we have exchanged our freedom for life in a prison from which we are unable to escape.

Another early figure who approached the problems of society with an extremely broad approach was Karl Marx, who preceded Weber by half a century. He was a German philosopher, economist, sociologist, journalist, and revolutionary socialist. He joined Weber along with other founders of sociology—such as Emile Durkheim and Georg Simmel—in his deep concern about the many problems linked to the early industrialization of Europe, with the movement from farm to factory.

In his early work in the 1840s, Marx focused on the experiences of the individual worker, especially on assembly lines. He was much concerned with the worker's experience of "alienation" or isolation within a setting that emphasized conformity to the hierarchical relationships among factory owners, managers and workers. Marx explained the nature of alienation in this excerpt from an essay:

> We have now considered the act of alienation of practical human activity, labour, from two aspects: (1) the relationship of the worker to the product of labour as an alien object which dominates him…[**physical alienation**]
>
> (2) the relationship of labour to the act of production within labour. This is the relationship of the worker to his own activity as something alien and not belonging to him…This is self-alienation as against the above-mentioned alienation of the thing…[**personality alienation**]
>
> Since alienated labour: (1) alienates nature from man; and (2) alienates man from himself, from his own active function, his life activity; so it alienates him from (3) the species…For labour, life activity, productive life, now appear to man only as means for the satisfaction of a need, the need to maintain his physical existence…free, conscious activity is the species-character of human beings. [**biological alienation**]
>
> (4) A direct consequence of the alienation of man from the product of his labour, from his life activity and from his species-life, is that man is alienated from other men. [**social alienation**] (1844/1964: 125-127, 129; boldface added)

Marx's broad focus on physical, personality, biological and social structures is a lesson for all of us who have become victims of our specialized and isolated way of life.

It is this very isolation of the individual from all of these structures that is much the same as his or her imprisonment, following Weber's image of the "iron cage." For what does prison achieve if not the alienation of the individual from physical nature, from himself, from his biological nature, and from others?

Modern social scientists have supported the early Marx's analysis of the power of persisting hierarchies in the workplace that shape the entire life of the worker, applying these ideas to society as a whole. They have equally supported the existence of narrow specialization coupled with patterns of conformity that are additional keys to our present-day behavior.

At the same time, social scientists generally have found severe limitations to much that Marx wrote in his later work, such as the idea that a violent revolution is essential to take power away from owners and place that power in the hands of workers. There is also the view that, despite Marx's intellectual breadth, he was dogmatic about the truth of his ideas rather than the follower of a scientific method that is open to new evidence that might contradict one's ideas.

Yet Marx was not alone in his dogmatic orientation, as is illustrated by this story of a Buddhist monk told many years ago. A merchant leaves his son to take care of his residence while going on a business trip. He returns to discover that bandits had entered his town and burned his house down to the ground. Searching for his son, he discovers a body so badly burned that it is beyond recognition. Grief-stricken, he assumes it is his son's body.

Actually, the bandits had taken his son to be a slave. Years later his son manages to escape from his captors and returns to the house that his father had rebuilt. He knocks on the door, begging his father to open it, crying, "Father, I am here!" But his father answers, "Go away, my son is dead."

Over the years, his father had become an embittered and lonely man who kept to himself. He assumes that some young man in the neighborhood is mocking his grief. His son continues to cry out for his father to open the door, but the door remains closed, and the son finally goes away. The Buddhist monk then told the moral of the story: "A closed mind fails to recognize possibilities."

We suggest that almost all of us have closed our minds to the incredible power

of the individual to help change the world as well as to achieve much deeper meaning in everyday life. Granting that we do not experience daily work on an assembly line, we nevertheless experience patterns of persisting hierarchy, conformity, and narrow specialization throughout our everyday lives. Recall, for example, what happened to Tom at the age of 7 in his Sunday school. Those kinds of experiences that we all have drastically limit our possibilities for developing an optimistic vision for self and world.

...

If we look historically to changes from optimism toward pessimism, World War I marked a fundamental change, taking us from the utopian visions of the 19th Century to the dystopias of the 20th Century. Donald McQuarie has analyzed the decline of optimistic images in fiction occurring during this period (1980). For example, the 19th Century works of Jules Verne and H. G. Wells were influenced by many years of unprecedented scientific and technological achievements.

But they were followed by books such as Aldous Huxley's *Brave New World* (1946), George Orwell's *Nineteen-Eighty-Four* (1949), Ray Bradbury's *Fahrenheit 451* (1953), Anthony Burgess' *A Clockwork Orange* (1962), and Kurt Vonnegut's *Slaughterhouse-Five* (1969). More recently, we've had Margaret Atwood's *The Handmaid's Tale* (1985) and Suzanne Collins' *The Hunger Games* (2008).

Contemporary dystopian films abound, with *Soylent Green* (1973), *Escape from New York* (1981), *Blade Runner* (1982), *The Matrix* (1999), and *Atlas Shrugged* (2011) as a very few examples.

These dystopian novels and films are about human problems. They indicate a widespread failure to achieve the positive perspective that a science of human behavior demands.

McQuarie concludes his analysis by posing a question about contemporary science fiction. He saw a contradiction between its professed ideals of freeing the human imagination and its actual timidity in envisioning fundamental social change that points in a utopian direction. How is this to be explained?

His answer to his own question builds on theories of the Italian Marxist, Antonio Gramsci (1971), who turned Marx on his head. Instead of Marx's emphasis on the economic system as much of the basis for the dominance of the ruling class, he saw the exercise of "cultural hegemony" or "ideological dominance" as their basic tool. McQuarie looks to modern culture as yielding science fiction's timidity:

> The corruption of the classical utopian vision in modern science fiction is but an aspect of the general stifling of ideological debate in 20th-century American political and cultural life. The cold hand of corporate and technocratic domination extends it holds...to every sector of modern intellectual life, creating a cultural wasteland which is incapable of nurturing works of any truly transcendental vision (249).

Gramsci and McQuarie do not abandon Marx's emphasis on the existence of economic and political domination by the ruling class. Rather, they shift their emphasis to what they see as a more contemporary battleground. This struggle is taking precedence over economic and political warfare.

It has much to do with what happens on television, on the internet, and in newspapers and magazines. It is a battle over the consciousness of the individual. It is not just the timidity of science fiction writers that is at stake, but also limits on the imagination for the rest of us.

Instead of developing our own unique ideas, we all learn patterns of conformity in our thoughts and action.

...

Here is a story that Tom Savage told me which can help us understand the focus on conformity within our present way of life. It is about an experience that took place in one of our national parks, never identified, but it sounded like Yellowstone.

The Fergusons (the name has been changed to protect the guilty party) had spent a week in nature's cathedral of tall trees, waterfalls and lakes. Camping, backpacking, horseback riding, the adventure had ended on a high note, but now it was time to go home.

Leaving the camp site and pulling up to the main highway, Mr. Ferguson saw a long line of cars coming, with only a small opening behind the lead vehicle. He took advantage of the space, and gunned his car into it.

Ferguson, a minister, was amused by the sign on the lead vehicle, which read, "Follow me," an expression that Jesus himself had used. Indeed, his own congregation had followed him, paralleling the followers of Jesus.

But soon, an uneasy feeling had crept over Reverend Ferguson. Had not he and his family earlier followed a similar "Follow me" vehicle going to some bear or bird-watching activity? Now, on a curve, the "Follow me" vehicle had turned off down a dirt road and disappeared. And that line of cars was now following the Fergusons, who were on their way home.

Realizing the possible mistake he had made, Reverend Ferguson's first response was a natural one—he panicked and increased his speed. But so did the line of cars. He then slowed down to a crawl, yet the other cars did the same.

Finally, spotting a scenic viewing overlook, Reverend Ferguson pulled off the road into the parking lot, when a Park Ranger Jeep pulled in, looking for his lost safari. Now it was the minister who was the one who had been "saved" from having chosen to get behind a vehicle reading "Follow me."

As the Park Ranger led the other drivers back to the appointed site for the nature program, the drivers who passed the good minister provided expressions of annoyance, amusement, frustration, anger, and a finger gesture that cannot be interpreted in polite society.

The moral has to be what Ralph Waldo Emerson wrote: "Whoso would be a man must be a nonconformist." But where are the nonconformists in our world? Robert Kennedy gave a speech in Cape Town, South Africa, that included these words: "For every ten men who are willing to face the guns of an enemy, there is only one willing to brave the disapproval of his fellow, the censure of his colleagues, the wrath of his society."

...

Our conformity to the wishes and behavior of our leaders includes going along with their narrow specialization, which in turn yields ignorance about how to solve problems. This lack of understanding was illustrated by the well-known sociological theorist Robert K. Merton in an article "The Unanticipated Consequences of Purposive Social Action" (1936), describing results far from what had been planned.

The historian Hilmar S. Rauschenbusch followed up on Merton's analysis by uncovering many major historical instances of such unanticipated consequences (1969).

For example, the early Christians allied themselves with the Roman Empire to give their religion a firmer foundation; this resulted in Christianity's absorbing an elitist orientation, conflicting with the emphasis by Jesus on equality.

After World War I, the allies sought to keep Germany weak by collecting large indemnities and having the nation accept sole guilt; a national resentment allowed Hitler to build a powerful war machine, and start World War II.

In attempting to deprive blacks of their civil rights, some Southern sheriffs used cattle prods and police dogs to enforce unjust laws. This was picked up by television cameras, resulting in a moral outcry ensuring the passage of civil rights laws.

…

We like to think that contemporary education has given us important knowledge that takes us far beyond the ignorance of peoples in early times when writing had not even been invented. We celebrate education as an unmixed blessing. And present-day education has indeed given us much to be thankful for, when we look to our achievements, such as in medicine, agriculture, housing, transportation, communication, and knowledge of human behavior.

Yet we fail to understand the world of orality—before the invention of writing—that we literates have lost, as described by Walter J. Ong in his *Orality and Literacy* (1982). There we can see the illiterate as being superior to us in many ways. This is the world of the direct and moment-to-moment perception of people and things, of emotional reaction to those experiences, and of immediate action as a result.

To illustrate, we might look to the time of Julius Caesar near the beginning of the Christian era, a time much closer to the world of orality than our present time of literacy.

Following Shakespeare's play, Marc Anthony was able to sway with his oratory the crowd of Romans to avenge Caesar's murder. We see there the power of rhetoric to capture people's emotions and actions.

Rhetoric was an early staple of formal education, but it is hardly taught today within our era of literacy, granting that some schools have debating teams and courses in rhetoric. This emphasis follows the oral tradition of helping students move beyond a passive understanding of knowledge into active use of their understanding as the basis for making important choices.

Reading and writing have largely taken us away from such emotional experiences that in turn are the basis for decisive action.

Today, just as we have been taught to suppress our emotions, we have learned to become Hamlets who remain unable to act when actions are desperately required. "To be, or not to be?" Should we, or shouldn't we? What will others say? Will we feel guilty? Will we be doing the right thing? Is it safer simply to let others act in our place?

Think of the inaction of our social scientists, guided by literacy, who have come to see themselves as so specialized as to cede to politicians, psychotherapists, social workers, educators, and journalists the sphere of action. For supposedly they are the ones who know how to act.

But never mind that the knowledge of politicians and others is not broad enough to provide the basis for effective action. Never mind that they do not read the studies of social scientists.

Readers may recall that our focus in the foregoing pages of Chapter 1 has been on one part of the see-saw metaphor. Its heading, "Conformity to Our Present Way of Life," emphasizes the static nature of this recreational structure. Being fixed to the ground, it prevents people from moving upward, or developing a vision of continually improving their behavior.

We now turn to the second part of this metaphor. There is the frustration suggested by one's movement down that might suggest behavior such as lowering one's self-esteem, and giving way to depression and even suicide. There is also the aggression implied by moving up and putting one's partner down. This might suggest behavior such as bullying or abusing others, racism and other isms, and even terrorism and warfare.

FRUSTRATION AND AGGRESSION

We have emphasized in the Introduction the importance of *kaizen*, or continuing improvement, as a basis for an evolutionary vision for self and society. Yet we do not argue that a high expectation or elevated vision for such developments is always the best way to actually achieve continuing improvement. To illustrate, the sociologist Richard Farson has attempted to explain why good marriages are often in greater jeopardy than bad ones (1977).

It is in good marriages, Farson argues, that expectations for the behavior of one's partner are heightened, by contrast with bad marriages. Given that situation, it is much easier for one's partner to fall below those expectations, yielding frustration and conflict. If expectations are low, as in bad marriages, the behavior of the couple will be more likely to conform to them. Thus, it is the size of the gap between one's expectations or aspirations and their fulfillment that is the basis for either frustration or a sense of personal fulfillment.

This same idea is used by corporate executives and politicians. Executives are careful not to predict high earnings in the event that profits fall below those expectations, yielding a large expectations-fulfillment gap. If there is no such gap, they will be seen as excellent managers.

Similarly, politicians generally are careful not to make predictions about increases in their country's Gross National Product that will later fall below what actually occurs, and for the same reasons. Visions are most valuable when they motivate their actual fulfillment. They can cause serious problems, however, when they result in a large aspirations-fulfillment gap.

An illustration of the contrast between our high expectations and total failure to fulfill them is found in a story told by comedian Bob Newhart. It is about a nuclear submarine that went on a six-month shakedown cruise, an endurance test for both crew and equipment. Just before returning to base, the captain summoned his crew together to reflect on the voyage's record-breaking accomplishments.

"Men," he said, "this is a time for celebration. On the whole, with admittedly a few minor exceptions, this mission may be considered a success. On our first emergency crash-dive test, we submerged in record-breaking time, and I think it only fitting that we stand for a moment of respectful silence, appreciating the two sailors we had to leave topside in order to establish our record.

"In the annals of medical history at sea, I think that the emergency appendectomy Seaman Johnson performed on Seaman Winters went above and beyond the exceptional. The fact that we later learned Seaman Winters' appendix had already been removed some two years earlier in no way detracts from this almost successful operation. And whatever organ Seaman Johnson did remove from Seaman Winters probably would have had to come out sooner or later anyway.

"Now, a few words about the mutiny. Guys, if you had problems or gripes, you could have come to me. My door was always open. And, I'd like that door returned along with my missing First Officer, Lieutenant Dawson.

"Finally, welcome home. It's been a long and—I know at times—hard journey. But remember how proud we were when we sank those three Japanese freighters and that tanker? True, we've been at peace with Japan for some twenty years, but it still stands as a record peace-time sinking.

"As for our shelling of a California beach vacation resort, that episode was blown way out of proportion by a too-literal and liberal fake news organization.

"Again, men, congratulations. Mission accomplished. That is all. You are dismissed."

...

A fundamental problem with our bureaucratic vision is that it directs our attention away from ourselves and toward external phenomena. It is an outward orientation, by contrast with an inward-outward perspective or pattern of perception. As a result, this orientation replaces any effort by the individual to develop a vision of his or her own continuing improvement.

For example, in school we learn about how to read and write, what happened in history, and the way government works. We are taught how to add, subtract, multiply and divide, explore the nature of the universe, identify the chemical elements, and to understand biological evolution.

But we fail to learn much about ourselves, the most complex creature throughout the known universe. How can we come to understand the nature of our fears and hates, our feelings of guilt and shame, or, conversely, what causes us to develop confidence and love, or self-acceptance and pride? How do we become motivated to enter the arena of action, by contrast with sitting back and waiting for others to do what we should do ourselves?

Reader, think of your own experiences in everyday life. How frequently do you perceive your own body versus the world around you? How frequently do you regard your own past or future, versus external tasks that must be done? How frequently do you watch television, surf the internet, go to movies, versus explore the nature of your own capacities and abilities, where you have been in the past, what you might do in the future?

An outward orientation is further illustrated by comparing our grades in school to the grades of other students, or to the class average. By contrast, there is the inward orientation of comparing one's grades with one's own previous grades.

Conformity is the very nature of our way of life, rather than autonomy, where we learn to develop our own unique ideas and practices. But, like lemmings, we have learned to follow our leaders, no matter whether they take us over the cliff.

Reader, think back to Socrates' claim that the unexamined life is not worth living, or Funakoshi's belief that in karate we should first know ourselves before knowing others. Or recall Erich Fromm's belief that the failure of modern culture is due to our failure to learn to love ourselves.

George Gurdjieff, an Armenian philosopher, can help us to understand just how large an outward perspective is with little or no attention to oneself, compared to one's personal development or evolution. He traveled extensively throughout the Middle East, Africa, and Central Asia. One of Gurdjieff's students, P. D. Ouspensky, recorded and explained Gurdjieff's ideas in his *The Fourth Way* (1971).

Ouspensky believed that when we try to think of ourselves we can maintain that focus for only a very short time before our minds move toward external phenomena. He explains:

> If we begin to study ourselves we first of all come up against one word which we use more than any other and that is the word "I". We say "I am doing", "I am sitting", "I feel", "I like", "I dislike" and so on. This is our chief illusion...we consider ourselves one...when in reality we are divided into hundreds of different "I"s...
>
> So in self-observation...generally you do not *remember yourself*...because you cannot remember yourself, you cannot concentrate, and...you have no will. If you could remember yourself, you would have will and could do what you liked...You may sometimes have will for a short time, but it turns to something else and you forget about it...we become too absorbed in things, too lost in things... (3-4, 12)

Ouspensky's analysis emphasizes just how difficult it would be for us to move away from our outward orientation. We are fooled into believing that we are unitary beings, that there is such a thing as an integrated "I," when in fact we are shattered beings. As a result, we become Hamlets who remain unable to build up the motivation to take decisive actions on the problems we face. Our patterns of conformity, with their outward orientation, have completely taken over our lives.

Yet Ouspensky believed that we can learn to abandon our outward orientation with the help of education. He follows our own vision of the human being as possessing enormous potential for continuing personal development or evolution. This is a rare perspective, yet we are convinced of the existence of our possibilities based on both our studies and our personal experiences.

We do not expect you, our readers, to accept this idea simply because we believe it. Instead, we are convinced that the full body of ideas that we present in this book will open up this possibility for you. What is essential, however, is that you test these ideas within your own everyday behavior.

Ouspensky's criticism of our educational institutions is profound. They teach us about history and society, about the sciences, the humanities, and the technologies, but they fail to teach us about ourselves. How are we to solve our own personal problems? How are we to deal with our negative emotions? How are we to learn how to relate closely to other people? Ouspensky argues that we are complicated beings, and that we cannot rely on instincts to guide our behavior.

Just like actors on stage, we are always playing a role. We are males or females, husbands or wives, parents or children, teachers or students, workers or bosses. We lose sight of ourselves, succumbing to conformity to what we see as the role's requirements. Our "I" and our will or emotional strength disappear in favor of what those roles demand.

...

An experience of Tom Savage in his role as a law-enforcement officer can help us appreciate and understand the impact of an outward-oriented bureaucratic education, which compromises people's ability to examine and develop their own lives.

Two alcoholic parents went out for an evening of drinking, leaving their four-year-old son in charge of a sleeping six-month-old baby in its crib, which the boy was not tall enough to see the baby. The baby became entangled in pillow and bedclothes, smothered, and died.

When the parents returned and found the child dead, they turned on the small boy, saying, "You've killed your baby sister!" The poor kid fell to the floor, wailing in despair, which is how the EMT's found him.

Can we but wonder if this boy will be scarred for life by the guilt of this memory? And what punishment would be most appropriate for these irresponsible parents? We leave it to our readers to decide.

Those parents, addicted to alcohol, were unable to examine their own lives. Escaping from their own problems, they turned outward and became addicted to alcohol.

...

Another illustration can back up Ouspensky's analysis. In a book entitled *Opera Bloopers*, two extras, playing the role of guards, having missed the final dress rehearsal, asked the conductor what they were to do at the end of the opera. They were simply instructed to follow the lead singer.

As a result, when Tosca leaped into the Tiber the two guards obediently jumped in right behind her. They saw themselves as playing a role, just like we all do, submerging any personal vision of their own behavior. A standing ovation was the reward for their sense of duty, for the audience was outwardly oriented no less than the actors.

Although this story is amusing, it indicates extremely serious problems throughout contemporary societies. This very outward orientation is much of the basis for patterns of frustration and aggression. If, then, our outward perspective is central to our way of life, then frustration and aggression are also built into the very nature of society.

As a result, any specialized approach to eliminating bullying, racism or any other pattern of aggression is doomed to be quite limited in its effects. For nothing less than absolutely fundamental changes in the individual—such as moving to adopt an inward-outward orientation—will do.

Also, specialized efforts to confront emotional problems like frustration will equally be limited in their effectiveness. For those efforts will not be able to reverse something as fundamental as our outward orientation.

This analysis calls into question society's many specialized efforts to solve personal problems, such as deep frustration or even suicide, and world problems of aggression against others or even war and terrorism. The educator Ivan Illich had much to say about this immense failure of society to solve our basic problems in *Deschooling Society* (1971):

> Many students, especially those who are poor, intuitively know what the schools do for them. They school them to confuse process and substance. Once these become blurred, a new logic is assumed: the more treatment there is, the better are the results; or, escalation leads to success.

> The pupil is thereby "schooled" to confuse teaching with learning, grade advancement with education, a diploma with competence, and fluency with the ability to say something new. His imagination is "schooled" to accept service in place of value.

> Medical treatment is mistaken for health care, social work for the improvement of community life, police protection for safety, the rat race for productive work. Health, learning, dignity, independence, and creative endeavor are defined as little more than the performance of the institutions which claim to serve these ends, and their improvement is made to depend on allocating more resources to the management of hospitals, schools, and other agencies in question. (1-2)

Illich's concept of "schooling" is much the same as our own idea of "conformity." He claims that such schooling, or conformity to believing that specialized institutions are really solving problems when in fact they are not, leads to a "growing frustration gap" between people's expectations and their actual fulfillment.

He also cuts across the usual political divides that separate fascist, democratic and socialist societies from one another. Instead, he sees them all as creating schooled or conformist societies. For Illich, these societies all enforce a "hidden curriculum" that "bureaucracies guided by scientific knowledge are efficient and benevolent."

We see Illich's analyses as exactly on the mark. Where he fell short is in failing to envision a way to actually "deschool" society by offering a practical direction for moving away from our present way of life. This is exactly what we attempt to do in this book. We are convinced that not only can we learn more and more about the failure of our present patterns of behavior, but we can also learn ever more about an alternative way of life that can increasingly solve personal and world problems.

. . .

Staying with the overriding importance of education, while not excluding non-traditional education—such as by means of television and the internet—the Brazilian educator Paolo Freire can add to Ouspensky's and Illich's ideas. He contrasted "life-affirming" and "humanizing" pedagogy with education that mirrors "oppressive society" in his *Pedagogy of the Oppressed* (1972).

Freire saw such a society as using this kind of education: (1) the teacher teaches and the students are taught; (2) the teacher knows everything and the students know nothing; (3) the teacher talks and the students listen—meekly; and (4) the teacher confuses the authority of knowledge with his own professional authority, which he sets in opposition to the freedom of the students.

We might think of the impact of this kind of education on students' ability to develop an optimistic vision of their future. Instead, they are taught to continue seeing a world oriented to hierarchy, conformity, and limited knowledge as their only alternative. Still further, they learn an outward orientation, frustration, and aggression against themselves or others, for those phenomena are also tied closely to their bureaucratic way of life.

Of course, a good deal of education follows a far less hierarchical approach, and we can be grateful for that. Within many schools we have dedicated teachers who are committed to help their students move toward fulfilling their potentials. This occurs at all levels of education and in all countries. However, the oppressive type of education that Freire described remains all too common.

. . .

If we look to where teachers and the rest of us learn to adopt their commitment to a very limited vision of our possibilities, we find a great deal of it in advertising that inserts itself throughout our everyday experiences. Despite prevalent beliefs that we rise above being influenced by advertising, advertisers generally succeed in brainwashing us. Why else would corporations continue to spend billions of dollars in flooding the mass media with news about the wonders of their products?

John Berger examined the impact of advertising on us in his BBC television series and in a book based on that series, *Ways of Seeing* (1985). He found that advertising and publicity steal our love for ourselves, and then offer it back for the price of the product.

Yet viewers or readers are never allowed to actually recover love of themselves even if they buy the product. For they are continually bombarded by many other messages throughout the day that also steal away their self-love, and they certainly cannot buy all of the products that are advertised. This works to destroy the viewer's or reader's self-confidence no less than love of self.

Thus, one's perceptual experiences watching television and the internet, or reading newspapers and magazines, succeeds in shaping our ideas, emotions and actions. Just as our way of life with its outward orientation emphasizes the individual's insignificance, so does advertising accomplish the same thing. For it is the advertised products that are significant, and we are nothing unless we buy them.

...

Following Berger, not only is our personal development stolen from us, but advertising points us away from building on our democratic heritage. It teaches us that we are actually making a meaningful choice when we buy Coca-Cola rather than Pepsi-Cola, and all the while ignore behavior that can actually make a difference.

As for what happens to the choice between voting and not voting in a primary election, between communicating or not communicating to a Congressional Representative, between joining or not joining a march that demonstrates what one believes, between running and not running for a public office to start a movement opposing injustices, forget all of that. For one's choice of Coca-Cola over Pepsi-Cola becomes our substitute for democracy.

...

A story can yield further insight into our present situation. A compulsive gambler dies and finds himself in a magnificent casino where every day he wins at any game he plays. In a short period of time he becomes bored. Talking to an angel, he says, "Frankly, I think I'd like to go to the other place, and the angel says, "This is the other place."

How can one develop genuine emotional commitment to choices that are actually important for oneself and for society if one continues to emphasize one's choice of a Snickers bar over a Three Musketeers, or Bounty roll of paper over Viva?

This insight is particularly relevant to the situation of all those individuals who have retired and have failed to develop new interests that have taken the place of their previous jobs. Their boredom is perhaps not so different from hell. And with limited vision of the future, one's emotional development and ability to solve problems of importance become limited as well.

Are we, then, destined to remain with our drastically limited vision of our own potential as well as the future of society?

Some have observed that boredom is the most important emotional problem of the human race. Of course, there are other negative emotions, such as pessimism, hate, shame, guilt, fear, despair, anxiety, unhappiness, disappointment and sorrow. Yet perhaps boredom takes the cake, for it reveals nothing less than the failure to develop any powerful emotion that drives one to act. Boredom reveals what modern society has done to us: made us little more than consumers who have learned to shop until we drop.

Is it possible for us to envision a way of life where we move away: From pessimism toward optimism?

From hate toward love? From shame toward pride?

From guilt toward self-acceptance? From fear toward confidence?

From despair toward hope? From anxiety toward serenity?

From unhappiness toward happiness? From disappointment toward satisfaction? From sorrow toward joy?

Perhaps most importantly, away from boredom toward passion?

We know that such movement from negative toward positive emotions is most desirable. Yet our education has failed to teach us how to achieve this. Such a fundamental failure has received almost no attention.

We continue to fiddle while Rome is burning.

...

Lewis Carroll's novel, *Alice's Adventures in Wonderland* (1865/1993), illustrates a wide range of our problems. It provides us with a fun-filled satirical description of an adventure that takes us to a place never before imagined. Carroll employs his metaphors to take aim at education, politics and literature in Victorian England, making use of strange anthropomorphic animal characters.

What does it take to make people want to grow up? This witty and nonsensical tale begins with Alice falling down a hole because she was curious. That makes her a seeker, looking for some of life's answers.

Of course, suppose that you were to see a white rabbit wearing a waistcoat, who is constantly checking his pocket watch while at the same time exclaiming, "I'm late! I'm late for a very important date." Then perhaps you, too, would wonder what is going on and be willing to pursue your own curiosity.

If you joined Alice in her pursuit of the rabbit, you would enter a most wondrous fantasy land and learn things along the way. For, you see, one of the central themes of the book is your finally having to "grow up."

The first thing we become aware of is that this Wonderland seems to be a world turned upside down and all mixed up. Adults are silly, arbitrary, and mindless, displaying bad and often incomprehensible thoughts and behavior.

Children, on the other hand, are presented as unprejudiced, charming, and innocent. The author has obviously never read William Golding's *Lord of the Flies.*

Alice finds herself in a long hall with many locked doors. "Curiouser and curiouser," she is overheard to remark. To become the right size in order to gain entrance to these doors, she has to either drink something (to grow) or eat something (to shrink) before proceeding. I was reminded of the rock-and-roll song, "The Green Door." Some poor guy wants to join the party fun going on behind him, but no one will allow him in.

Alice, frustrated with her own lack of success at the doors, begins to cry. This creates a pool of tears through which she must now swim.

Finally reaching the shore, her task is to get dry. A Dodo bird recommends joining a Caucus Race, which consists of everyone running around in a circle with no apparent winner. She has received boring and meaningless advice that is so dry that it does the trick.

Next, Alice comes upon a caterpillar sitting on a mushroom smoking a hookah. The caterpillar's smoke rings form letters that confront Alice with three of life's most profound questions: "Where are you? Why are you? Who are you?"

Regarding the last question, Alice is experiencing an identity crisis. She had to say that she wasn't quite sure just who she was because she had been so many different sizes that particular morning.

On one occasion, she had grown so very tall, she had disturbed a pigeon's nest with eggs in it atop a tree. And when Alice admitted that she rather enjoyed eating eggs, the pigeon accused Alice of being a serpent, which of course she was not.

And then there was the question of time regarding who one was. For certainly at age twelve one would not be the same as at seventeen, let alone at twenty-five, or God forbid, seventy.

Now, when eating one side or the other of this particular mushroom upon which the caterpillar sat, Alice was told it would make all the difference of who she was.

Harvard professor Timothy Leary gave a similar warning. Yet, he recommended the use of controlled substances as a vehicle for expanding one's consciousness. His LSD experiments promised to take one on a trip to another astral plane. So, too, was the message of the Beatles' LSD song, "Lucy in the Sky with Diamonds."

Tom was personally very sad to learn that one of his favorite pop songs, "Bridge Over Troubled Waters," also had a drug solution for personal problems. Just what was the "bridge" to help us over our troubled times? "Sail on silver girl, sail on by, your time has come to shine." In the 1960s in New York, the street vernacular for a syringe was a silver girl. In other words, a heroin fix would help you over your troubled waters.

A former girlfriend had said her use of drugs might be naughty but was nice. When she died of a drug overdose, her words seem to have lost some of their profundity and power. When addiction becomes excess, excess usually means "too much." English comedian Anna Russell makes this point: "When you do something too much, even if you think it is nice, it is too much!"

On his *You Bet Your Life* television show, Groucho Marx also agreed that "too much" can be a problem. A female contestant revealed that she had ten children, for she and her husband just loved to make love. Groucho responded, "Well, I love to smoke, but I at least take the cigar out of my mouth on occasion."

One of Alice's more bazaar experiences occurred at the home of a Duchess. Her cook used too much pepper. This caused a nearby baby to sneeze violently, only to be beaten for something that wasn't his fault.

While attending the stupidest tea party she'd ever experienced, hosted by a Mad Hatter, Alice recalled the Cheshire Cat stating that in Wonderland everyone was quite mad. How true. At the tea party, riddles were asked that had no possible answers, possibly preparing one for a later class in Philosophy 101.

Finally, we arrive at the Queen's croquet grounds. Some gardeners, who have mistakenly planted white rose bushes, are now trying to correct their mistake by furiously painting them red, the Queen's favorite color. When the Queen shows up and discovers their mistake, she bellows, "Off with their heads," her favorite command.

Now Alice is asked if she would enjoy playing a game of croquet. Having no real choice, she agrees. The game is one of total chaos. Unmanageable flamingoes are the mallets, hedgehogs serve as balls, and playing cards have become wickets, which run around to make sure that all of the Queen's balls score. In short, the game was fixed, just as what happens to us so many times when we become victims of unjust systems.

Alice angers the Queen by questioning the rules of this unfair game, and is sentenced to stand trial. The Queen wants to sentence her first, and then proceed with the trial. Alice points out that this would be unjust, so she is able to avoid punishment.

The story ends when Alice realizes that all the creatures in Wonderland are "nothing but a pack of playing cards." It was time to wake up from her dream and join the adult world.

We can easily see the events in Wonderland as metaphors for the events in present-day society:

Just as the Queen arranges to win the game of croquet, so do the wealthy use their influence to widen the gap between the rich and the poor.

Just as the Queen wants the sentence before the trial, so we have discovered that many men and women of color have already been prejudged before appearing in court.

Just as a baby has been set up to start sneezing with all of the pepper present, which is the condition of its environment, so society has created situations which result in citizens being punished for actions that were not their fault.

If all the creatures in Wonderland are "nothing but a pack of playing cards," then have we, too, been caught up in nothing but a game with no winners?

If Alice could not answer the question of who she was, then do we all fail to understand the nature of our own potentials?

If Alice's journey in Wonderland allows her to avoid facing the adult world, then do we all fail to face our own reality?

When the pigeon erroneously accuses Alice of being a serpent, she suggests our failure to use the scientific method.

When language in Wonderland is used to create riddles without answers, offering gibberish for conversation and bad advice for wisdom, so we also use language to both confuse and abuse.

It's time for Alice to wake up, and in so doing grow up. As should we all.

CHAPTER 2

The Solution: A Successful Evolutionary Vision

By now, we should all be aware of the enormous power of bureaucracy to drastically limit our vision of human possibilities.

It was essential for us to become aware of that power, for the initial requirement of the scientific method—which is nothing less than a problem-solving process—calls for an awareness of a problem.

It is that very awareness which motivates us to gain understanding of what causes the problem and how to address it effectively. Given that our central issue is the very destiny of the individual and society, we can rest assured of our potential for learning to develop enormous motivation to use that knowledge to take decisive actions.

If bureaucracy is powerful, then the scientific method is far more powerful, for it has succeeded in enabling us humans to change the world in fundamental ways over the past five centuries. When ordinary individuals with no advanced degrees learn that they have already been employing this method and can make use of its most effective tools, our ability to solve any and all problems will multiply.

The opening section of Chapter 2 introduces "The Interdisciplinary Scientific Method," building on our earlier insights.

Next, we present "The Power of Language." There we learn how key elements of language are much of the basis for the incredible effectiveness of that method.

We conclude with "Personal Productivity." When one gains awareness of the full power of this problem-solving tool in one's possession, then there is absolutely no limit to what can be accomplished.

INTERDISCIPLINARY SCIENTIFIC METHOD

We start with an image of a stairway, just as we envisaged a see-saw—with its up and down movement suggesting winners and losers—in introducing our vision of the nature of bureaucracy.

It is a problem-solving stairway, for each step that we climb yields progress toward the solution of a given problem.

The steps are wide enough to accommodate the entire human race, for everyone makes use of this procedure.

There is no limit to how far the stairway extends, for our double crisis of meaninglessness and threatening world problems is continually present and requires constant attention.

That stairway does not become narrower as it moves upward, so my climbing further does not result in less room for others.

By contrast with the see-saw, where my moving up requires my partner to move down, my climbing can help others. They can be encouraged by my ascent, and I can explain how I overcame obstacles.

The issues that the stairway addresses are extremely wide-ranging. They can include personal evolution—intellectual, emotional, and problem-solving ability— no less than improving solutions to the present world crisis.

This stairway, seen as a metaphor for personal and world evolution, is an important learning tool because it shares with other metaphors the ability to make visible what otherwise would remain invisible. As a result, we come to see more clearly just what is required to make an evolutionary journey.

...

Fred Polak—a Dutch sociologist and well-known futurist—believed in the enormous power of visions. After having studied the entire history of Western civilization (1961, 1973), he wrote: "The more powerful the image of the future is, the more powerfully it acts in determining the actual future" (1961, II: 341).

What, then, are the characteristics of such an image that make it effective? How effective, in the sense of promising to yield actual changes in society, is our own vision?

The contemporary sociologist Lawrence Busch based his doctoral dissertation (1974) on Polak's achievements. In an article following his dissertation, Busch focused on answering the question of "What conditions appear necessary to construct the future successfully, either as individuals, as organizations, or as a society" (1976: 29).

Key requirements for a successful image of the future that Busch discovered mesh with our own vision of how to move toward personal and world evolution.

First, an image must be broad or "holistic" in order to achieve widespread acceptance. Busch and Polak have been updated in this requirement for an influential vision by the sociologist Mary Romero in her *Introducing Intersectionality* (2018). She argues, for example, that race, class and gender yield interlocking and overlapping influences that cannot be ignored if one seeks to understand the complex problems within any one of these areas.

...

To match this requirement, there is our own emphasis on moving away from bureaucracy's narrow specialization with little integration of knowledge.

Readers may recall that it was C. Wright Mills who started me on my own interdisciplinary journey. His *The Sociological Imagination* (1959/2000) presented his broad vision that builds on the breadth of classical sociologists:

> The sociological imagination...is the capacity to shift from one perspective to another—from the political to the psychological; from examination of a single family to comparative assessment of the national budgets of the

world; from the theological school to the military establishment; from considerations of an oil industry to studies of contemporary poetry (7).

Readers might also recall the breadth of the five authors of this book, Our age range takes us from the 20s to the 80s. We include two sociologists with experience in the arts and the sciences, a former minister and sheriff lieutenant, someone in the field of medicine, and an economist.

Another requirement for a successful image that Polak and Busch advance is that it must promise to resolve basic problems within the existing order.

Our own emphasis on placing the full power of the scientific method in the hands of the individual points in this direction.

Polak and Busch also call for giving people workable procedures for making progress on the problems involved. Those procedures must be broad enough to include people's ordinary or mundane activities.

Our focus on extending the idea of *kaizen* or continuing improvement to the individual's behavior throughout his or her everyday life points in this direction.

Yet another demand for the success of a vision is that it is structured, just as a constitution yields a clear structure for people's behavior.

This book provides a structure. By including close attention to personality structure no less than social structure, it provides a broad resource that can help one solve personal and world problems.

...

The problems that we are addressing are so fundamental that they invoke the big "why" question that religion tries to answer. Why should we go on living? Why is life meaningful? Why should the human race continue to survive?

Here is a story Tom Savage told me about how these questions might be addressed within the context of religion. Just as an arena for scientific research is the laboratory, the place for religion's celebrations is the sanctuary. On one high holy day the children entered, twirling around, each holding a different letter, so that when put together they spelled "HAPPY HOLIDAY." The problem? One "Y" was missing.

The answer was provided by Carolyn Johnson, age 5. "Why" had to go to the bathroom. And when you have to go, you have to go. Missing in action, so to speak. Her late entrance brought a standing ovation. Searching for answers to life's basic questions is never easy. When found, it is cause for great rejoicing.

...

Given how important is the problem of moving society and the individual in an evolutionary direction at this time in history, and given the power of forces throughout society that stand in our way, we require as much understanding as possible. There is more that we can learn by turning to the efforts of Judge Louis C. Brandeis, who became a Justice of the Supreme Court.

Brandeis used a new type of legal document, that later came to be called the "Brandeis brief," in a 1908 court case challenging Oregon's requirement that employed women were to work very long hours. It included three pages of traditional legal citations and over one hundred pages of other materials: citations to articles, governmental reports, and other references. Those documents presented the results of social research that demonstrated the importance of a ten-hour limitation on women's working hours.

The result, in *Muller v. State of Oregon*, was the first Supreme Court ruling that accepted the legitimacy of a scientific examination of social conditions in addition to the legal precedents involved.

Louis Brandeis's vision of the role of the judiciary extended far beyond merely staying with precedents provided by past rulings. He saw society as undergoing basic changes, and he felt it important for the judiciary to take those changes into account.

He succeeded in following the ancient Japanese proverb: "A vision without action is a dream, and action without a vision is a nightmare." It was his Brandeis brief that yielded the action accompanying his vision as to what attorneys and justices should be doing. That action in turn strengthened his vision that looked to a changing future and not just to the past.

The Brandeis brief has been increasingly used in court cases, as illustrated in the *Brown v. Board of Education* case in 1954 that desegregated public schools. This was one of the very best examples ever experienced of the potential of the social sciences for helping to solve problems. Brandeis died in 1941. His ideas and work helped establish Brandeis University.

...

Thurgood Marshall, the first African American appointed to the Supreme Court, led a team of lawyers working with the NAACP Legal Defense and Educational Fund. They won that landmark 1954 *Brown v. Board of Education* case desegregating public schools.

Marshall and his group enlisted the support of social scientists who provided expert testimony supporting the conclusions of the doll tests introduced by two psychologists, Kenneth and Mamie Clark.

Their doll experiment involved children being presented with two completely identical dolls, but with one exception. One doll was white with yellow hair, and the other was brown with black hair. Children were then asked which one they would play with, which one is the nice doll, which one has the nicer color, and so on. The results showed a clear preference for the white doll among all the children in the study.

Such "self-hatred" was more acute among those attending segregated schools in Washington, D.C., than in integrated schools located in New York. Results, along with the testimony of social scientists and others, overturned a previous judicial ruling deciding that segregated schools could in fact deliver equally worthwhile education.

In a unanimous decision, Chief Justice of the Supreme Court Earl Warren declared that separate but equal education was unconstitutional, because it resulted in African American children developing "a feeling of inferiority as to their status in the community."

Marshall, like Brandeis, was no believer in the complete authority of judicial precedents. He once described his legal philosophy as this: "You do what you think is right and let the law catch up." He also followed the Brandeis brief in providing justification for what he thought was right by taking advantage of the knowledge of social scientists.

...

We can all learn to make use of available social science knowledge to address any problem whatsoever, just as Brandeis and Marshall did in their Supreme Court decisions. Yet it may surprise readers to learn that social scientists themselves are far more comfortable about developing knowledge than actually applying their understanding to confront problems.

It is true that some sociologists, such as Michael Burawoy (2008), have called for involvement in a "public sociology." It is equally the case that one of sociology's many sections centers on public sociology and sociological practice, which I co-founded years ago. Yet granting that change is afoot, the discipline as a whole is not as yet committed to the importance of entering the arena of the mass media. It is there that the full power of the social sciences can be brought to bear on our escalating social problems.

A recent featured essay in *Contemporary Sociology* calls attention to this failing. Monica Prasad, a Northwestern University professor who works with students in a problem-solving sociology workshop, called a spade a spade in examining the behavior of her colleagues (2018).

She cites exceptions to the rule of waiting for others to solve problems, like Burawoy (2005), Luft (2015), Pearson, et al. (2016) and Watts (2017). Yet she also describes several traps that sociologists generally fall into. There is "Describing and Complaining Rather than Solving."

A second way to avoid solutions is "Studying the Victims Rather than the Villains." By so doing, sociologists avoid presenting a full picture of the process that is actually causing the problem.

Yet another procedure often used is "Critiquing Other Solutions Rather than Providing New Solutions." Yet Prasad maintains that it is indeed possible to develop "a more ambitious sociology," which is what a great many sociologists want.

...

A more ambitious sociology might also return to the basics of social research so as to improve its scientific power. That would help not only sociologists and other social scientists but also the rest of us, who can make full use of the scientific method in confronting world no less than personal problems.

To this end, we might return to a sociological theorist who advanced an idea that remains to be pursued: Alvin W. Gouldner, in his *The Coming Crisis of Western Sociology* (1970), wrote these words at a time of great turbulence in society. It was during the war in Vietnam and followed the assassinations of John and Robert Kennedy and Martin Luther King:

> The historical mission of a Reflexive Sociology…would be to transform the sociologist, to penetrate deeply into his daily life and work, enriching them with new sensitivities, and to raise the sociologist's self-awareness to a new historical level…A Reflexive Sociology means that we sociologists must—at the very least—acquire the ingrained habit of viewing our own beliefs as we now view those held by others. (487, 493)

This focus on the individual sociologist follows our book's emphasis on the individual. Gouldner advances the idea of adding research on the individual investigator to the research that is currently conducted throughout the social sciences, with its emphasis on the group and society.

With such reflexive knowledge, the social scientist, as well as the layman, would gain the opportunity to learn the nature of his or her impact on those being studied, an impact known as the "investigator effect." Such knowledge is a fundamental requirement of the scientific method, yet it is almost universally absent among the myriads of published studies by social scientists.

How would this help? By strengthening the effectiveness of the scientific method, social scientists and the lay public would gain the chance to learn the nature of their own biases. For example, given their conformity to a bureaucratic way of life, are they failing to detect the negative impacts of that way of life on those whom they are studying as well as on themselves? As a result, are they failing to uncover the invisible disease that is much of the basis for the problematic visible symptoms they are investigating?

Further, without envisioning an alternative to our present way of life, is their research biased in the direction of failing to uncover such an alternative? Does this in turn lead to research conclusions with a pessimistic view of human possibilities?

There is a good reason why Gouldner's idea of a reflexive sociology has not been followed up. It is much the same reason why there has been no response to *Bringing Men Back In* (1964), the address by George C. Homans as President of the American Sociological Association.

We might add the lack of any answer to "The Oversocialized Conception of Man in Modern Sociology" (1961). This article by sociologist Dennis H. Wrong criticizes sociologists' emphasis on the power of society to shape the individual, with little consideration given to the individual's ability to resist such conformity and, indeed, shape society.

We can understand such behavior once we open up to the power of our bureaucratic way of life over everyone, including social scientists. Yet Gouldner, Homans and Wrong point us toward a solution. By "bringing men back in" and changing lay people's vision as well as the focus of social scientists, we move to increase the power of the scientific method. That is a path that can lead us all to uncover our own biases, and to work toward removing them.

. . .

An ancient legend can help us here. A woman had an only son whom she loved dearly, but he died suddenly, and she was overwhelmed with grief. She sought out the most learned man in the country, and pleaded with him to restore her son to life. He replied: "Yes, I can help you. But first you must bring me a handful of salt from a household that has never experienced death, not father, mother, sister, brother, friend or servant."

The woman left, going from house to house throughout the entire countryside, yet she found not a single household where no one had died. Returning at last to her advisor, she wept at her failure to offer him a handful of salt. He replied, "Death comes to everyone, for that is our fate. So, should your family be free of it? Go now and bury your son, remove from your eyes your tears, and fill your heart with cherished memories. Then you shall be free to live your own life, just as your loving son would have wished.

By learning to become aware of our limitations, we can gain the freedom to fulfill our own potentials. Just as the learned man freed the woman to accept her son's death so that she could gain the freedom to live her own life, so can we all learn to become aware of the enormous power over us of a present way of life teaching us all to follow the leader. Once this situation changes from its present invisibility to visibility, we become freer to change that way of life. By doing so, we can proceed to enlarge our freedom immeasurably.

HARNESSING LANGUAGE'S FULL POWER

The story of our learning to empower ourselves with the aid of the scientific method is incomplete without bringing forward the incredible power of language to multiply the effectiveness of that method. Let us not forget that it is our complex languages that sharply differentiate us humans from all other organisms throughout the known universe.

The enormous power of language was hinted at in the 1961 film, *The Miracle Worker*, which portrayed the learning of language by Helen Keller, the deaf and blind pupil of Anne Sullivan.

The crucial scene portrayed the two of them at a water pump, with Anne spurting water from the pump onto one of Helen's hands while tapping out finger symbols on her other hand. Helen later wrote in her autobiography: "I knew then that 'w-a-t-e-r' meant the wonderful cool something that was flowing over my hand. That living word awakened my soul, gave it light, hope, set it free!"

Our usage of language is central to our very development as human beings. Without language, Helen was lost to the world that we all experience. It is most difficult for us even to imagine what her experiences had been like before that day at the water pump. Without words for herself and the world around her, she had been drastically limited in every way. With language, she began to open up to her inner world as well as the full range of her everyday experiences.

Language's power is well illustrated when a politician tweets a reference to "lunch," but misspells it as "launch." The consequences could be deadly.

...

We can understand the importance of saying clearly what we mean from this story from the British comedian, Anna Russell. Acting in the role of President of a Women's Fine Art Group, she announced: "It is wonderful to see so many at our Fine Arts Program. As you know, our organization stands for the higher vision of life, expecting neither reward nor enjoyment. I'm here to introduce the artist for tonight's performance. Actually, this would be done by our program chairwoman, Mrs. Finestein. But she's awfully sorry she could not be with us tonight. She has been in bed all week with the doctor." Naturally, at that point the audience laughed. Anna continued, "I think you're very unkind. She's having a horrible time!"

...

Alfred Korzybski was a Polish engineer who developed profound insight into the failure of human beings to make much use of the potentials of language for helping us to address our deepest problems. The title of his basic book, *Science and Sanity* (1933), reveals his approach. It is knowledge from the sciences that we must turn to if we are to learn how to become sane human beings.

The book helped him launch a new field, general semantics. He then founded the present-day Institute of General Semantics, and succeeded in influencing a great many students.

Among them was Samuel I. Hayakawa, a former Senator from California. His *Language in Thought and Action* (1949) carried forward Korzybski's ideas. The quarterly journal *ETC* continues to contribute to the ideas within this field. It centers on developing our linguistic abilities as a basis for attempting to solve the fundamental problems of the human race.

For a popular and highly readable treatment of Korzybski's ideas, readers might turn to A. E. Van Vogt's two science fiction novels: *The World of Null-A* (1945/1970) and its sequel, *The Players of Null-A* (1948). The hero is Gilbert Gosseyn (pronounced "go sane"). He makes good use of Korzybski's principles to save both the Earth and our Milky Way galaxy from destruction by Enro the Red, the archvillain whose approach to language parallels our own simplistic usages.

...

Enro's problem, along with our own, is his focus on linguistic "dichotomy" without attention to "gradation." This yields stereotypical or comic-strip thinking, illustrated by classifying people into good versus evil, knowledgeable or ignorant, and strong or weak. By contrast, a gradational approach would see people as having degrees of moral behavior, knowledge, and strength.

Adolph Hitler's dichotomous orientation saw the Jews as completely evil and the Aryan race as totally good. For Hitler, it became essential to eliminate those who are evil so that good people will survive. By contrast, Socrates avoided such simple-minded caricatures. Instead, he saw humans gradationally, having degrees of personal development. For Socrates, it is crucial for people to increase their degree of understanding of self and world. Recall his claim that "the unexamined life is not worth living."

It is a focus on dichotomous thinking without attention to gradation that prevents Republicans and Democrats from compromising with each other. This two-valued approach is much of the basis for racism, sexism, ethnocentrism and ageism. Gradation, by contrast, corresponds to a scientific approach to human behavior and the world around us. We might think here of the number system that builds on the idea of gradation and is fundamental to mathematics and the physical sciences.

This is by no means to claim that any use of linguistic dichotomy is harmful and unscientific. Dichotomies are an essential part of all languages. Almost every word divides the world in two: what the word refers to, on the one hand, and everything else, on the other hand.

To illustrate the importance of dichotomy, this book is based on the dichotomy between a bureaucratic and an evolutionary way of life. We have also emphasized the dichotomies between an outward orientation and an inward-outward orientation. Further, we've focused on the dichotomy between sociologists' concentration on society, on the one hand, and on the individual and society, on the other hand.

Dichotomous thought can help us to develop our emotions through recognition of the negative impacts of the problem as well as the positive results from a solution. We have illustrated this approach by organizing this book into pairs of chapters, with those stressing human problems followed by those emphasizing human development.

...

Granting the positive aspects of dichotomous usage, a purely black-and-white approach to life, as illustrated by this story, gets in the way of our ability to solve problems:

A Jew, a Hindu, and a Christian Unitarian were traveling together to attend an Interfaith Conference in Chicago. On a lonely back road, their car broke down, and they had to ask a local farmer if he could provide shelter for one night. He said he could, but he only had room for two, so someone would have to sleep in the barn.

The Jew volunteered. Lights went out, but shortly there was a knock on the front door. "I can't sleep in the barn," said the Jew. "There is a pig in there, which is an offense to my religion."

"No problem," said the Hindu. "I'll go!" Lights out, but once again there was soon a knock on the front door. "I'm sorry, but there is a cow in the barn, sacred to my faith, and I can't stay there," said the Hindu.

"For heaven's sake," said the Unitarian. "My denomination has no such hang-ups." Lights out once more, but, again a knock at the front door, and there stood the pig and the cow.

What is crucial is that dichotomous thinking be accompanied by gradational thought. Thus, we do not abandon dichotomy. Rather, we add gradation to it. This is realistic in that we do not try to jump immediately from a deep problem to a total solution and, as a result, fall flat on our faces.

It is exactly an emphasis on gradational thought that is at the heart of Korzybski's and Van Vogt's approach. Yet they believed that people must undergo a substantial learning process in order to emphasize such thinking.

...

Gradational thought is fundamental to scientific inquiry. Charles Sanders Peirce, the American who developed the philosophical basis for the scientific method, noted the importance of such thought for the progress of science:

> There follows one corollary which itself deserves to be inscribed upon every wall of the city of philosophy: Do not block the way of inquiry. To set up a philosophy which barricades the road of further advance toward the truth is the one unpardonable offence in reasoning, as it is also the one to which metaphysicians have in all ages shown themselves most addicted. (1896/1955: 54)

Despite the importance of the field of general semantics in providing a direction for our linguistic development, it has largely omitted attention to an absolutely central element of language: metaphor. Metaphor uses what we perceive, or what is visible, to help us take into account what is invisible.

Allegories—metaphorical stories such as *The Wizard of Oz*—that can suggest ideals which contrast with our present ideals in everyday life—are central to the vast field of knowledge about human behavior that we refer to as the humanities. When social scientists attempt to exclude metaphors and allegories from their scientific efforts—as they presently do—they succeed in impoverishing their own efforts to fulfill the explanatory ideal of the scientific method.

Ralph Waldo Emerson believed in metaphor's huge role in human development. In his first significant essay, "Nature"—appearing in *The Essential Writings of Ralph Waldo Emerson* (1836/2000)—he gives us an overall understanding of the importance of metaphor in our lives. Consider these examples he used: "A rolling stone gathers no moss. A bird in the hand is worth two in the bush. A cripple in the right way will beat a racer in the wrong. Make hay while the sun shines. The last ounce broke the camel's back." Although they focus on quite specific experiences, each one teaches us something about human behavior in general.

Emerson succeeded in linking concrete experiences, largely tied to the physical and biological world rather than to man-made products, and human learning about how to solve problems. For example, "Make hay while the sun shines" suggests that we should act decisively when opportunities for making progress present themselves, and not delay or procrastinate. We should learn to "strike while the iron is hot," yet another metaphor for timely action before an opportunity is lost.

One way for readers to extend Emerson's approach is to use more and more of their perceptual experiences as potential metaphors. Indeed, everything that we perceive, and not just a limited range of natural objects, can help one develop oneself. For example, we can learn to perceive our own bodies as metaphors for our capacity for continuing personal development.

Further, anything whatsoever that I do can become a metaphor for my continuing improvement. This includes my interaction with others, my posture while walking, the time I spend watching television, my diet, and the thousand and one mundane activities that make up my daily experiences.

Metaphor, then, becomes a basic tool enabling one to move in an evolutionary direction. This requires that we have a vision of our personal development so that we can link our activities to that vision. Recall the biblical proverb: "Without a vision the people perish." We can add a new proverb: "Without an evolutionary vision, the people fail to develop."

Following the biologist Stephen Jay Gould, I am a learning animal, just like everyone else. By learning to make use of my everyday experiences as metaphors, I can continue to develop my understanding, emotional commitment, and ability to solve problems.

We may see this usage of language's dichotomous, gradational and metaphorical elements as procedures that strengthen one's ability to employ the scientific method in everyday life. Such behavior can enable one to learn to increase, over time, one's "personal productivity." The result can be nothing less than effectively confronting our double crisis of a meaningless life and increasing world problems. We will now explore the nature of this achievement.

PERSONAL PRODUCTIVITY

A story can help us to understand what we might achieve with this combination of language and the scientific method.

Giuseppe Verdi was commissioned to compose *Aida*, an opera for the grand opening of the Suez Canal, to be performed at the recently dedicated new opera house in Cairo on Christmas Eve, 1871.

You probably know the story. Egypt is being invaded by an army from Ethiopia. The captain of the Egyptian guard is Radames, who is in love with Aida, an Ethiopian slave. Amneris, daughter of the Pharaoh, is in love with Radames, and fears Aida might be her rival. Radames' army defeats the Ethiopians, returning in triumph with treasure and slaves, one of whom is Aida's own father.

We turn now to our own story regarding the unanticipated performance of Charles "The Great." Charles Collins was physically a Greek god, and he knew it. But this was the early 60s with its biases and prejudices. And Charles was hampered by two inescapable realities: he was a black man and a rather effeminate gay male.

Coupled with this were his rather theatrical delusions of grandeur, and, well, you get the picture.

When a traveling opera company came to present *Aida*, they needed extras, and Charles, of course, was the first to sign up. The painful yet hilarious episode that followed just has to be told. Student volunteers were to be paid ten dollars a performance for carrying a spear. And a poor student could have a pretty good meal for ten dollars in the early 60s.

In the Triumphal March scene, Charles could just see how magnificent he would look carrying his spear behind Aida. But, because of his race and color, he was cast as an Ethiopian slave. Charles was not just offended, he was outraged.

Once on stage, however, he took advantage of his big unscripted moment. He had been told to lay prostrate, depicting a slave's subjugation. Instead, Charles rose to his knees, and with hands tightly clasped, his whole upper body dramatically weaving back and forth, Charles began a silent pantomime of a Southern black slave, pleading with Master Jack not to whip him anymore.

The attention of the whole audience was now on Charles, despite the best efforts of the singers who were trying to keep the focus on their own major roles. Charles' antics became so disruptive that the stage manager sent in two Egyptian guards to grab Charles and drag his black ass, as any sixties white Southern sheriff would have called it, off the stage.

At the end of Act II, the lead singers, Aida, Radames and Amneris, came out to take their respective bows, and were greeted with polite applause. Suddenly, out from the side curtain of the stage, burst Charles, who began dancing and prancing about, taking huge and exaggerated bows while at the same time blowing kisses to an audience now on its feet, cheering "Bravo" and "Go, man, go!"

The three lead singers, trying to maintain smiles, exited, but backstage they became furious over the outrage. Who in the hell was this nobody black slave taking away from what should have been their due?

Charles, however, now in his glory, continued to milk the moment, teasing and pleasing his audience for a full five minutes. Charles had thrived in those minutes, and he certainly knew now what it meant to be...somebody.

Those cheers illustrate the idea that we are all very much like Charles. We crave the belief that our lives are genuinely meaningful, that we deserve praise for who we are and what we have done. Granting that we do not have the opportunity to milk an audience for applause, those cheers were meant not only for Charles but also for the selves that the audience would have liked to be had they not succumbed to conformity.

Days later, the opera had pretty much been forgotten. But Charles' performance will be remembered forever.

Who among us would have, could have, dared to be so bold? Who has not sought to grasp the brass ring, or capture a moment in time to enjoy such celebrity? Who, except pop artist of Campbell's-soup-can fame, Andy Warhol, will challenge us to embrace our own much-deserved fifteen minutes of fame and glory? Thank you, Charles, for reminding us that when the world demands our obedience and conformity, instead of acting like lost sheep we can rise up to roar like lions.

Charles had illustrated nothing less than personal productivity, which may be defined very simply as the individual's solution of problems. This is exactly what the scientific method both calls for and enables its users to achieve. Charles had no Ph.D., but personal productivity requires none. The problem that he solved—at least for the time he remained on stage—was the personal recognition and meaningfulness that he and the rest of us crave.

As for the audience, they too achieved at least some degree of personal productivity. For once, they defied the rules of being subservient to applauding only recognized artists. They began applauding an ordinary individual not unlike themselves.

...

The idea of personal productivity takes us far beyond the narrow materialistic view of productivity that is encouraged throughout our economic system, where a nation's Gross National Product is the prime measure of its achievement.

By contrast, we can turn to the achievements of Walt Whitman. He is the poet best known for his "O Captain! My Captain!" which he wrote in response to the death of President Abraham Lincoln at the close of the American Civil War. He expressed his deep grief when his Captain had "Fallen cold and dead" just after "The ship has weather'd every rack, the prize we sought is won." Yet it was Whitman's *Leaves of Grass* (1892/2004) that illustrates his movement far beyond tragedy to express his faith in the individual:

> I celebrate myself, and sing myself,
> And what I assume you shall assume,
> For every atom belonging to me as good belongs to you
>
> . . . I believe in the flesh and the appetites,
> Seeing, hearing, feeling, are miracles, and each part and tag of me is a miracle.
>
> Divine am I inside and out, and I make holy whatever I touch or am touch'd from,
> The scent of these arm-pits aroma finer than prayer,
> This head more than churches, bibles, and all the creeds. (23, 44)

We can see in *Leaves of Grass* the same ideals about human possibilities that motivated the long lines of wagons moving out onto the Western plains under vast open skies to find a new home; that propelled the African-Americans moving up from the South to northern cities where they could work for decent wages; and that gave immigrants from Europe the courage to cross the Atlantic, escaping from poverty and oppression to see the Statue of Liberty and arrive in the land of their dreams.

Exactly what did Whitman "produce"? Did he invent some device that increased the market share of a company? Did he succeed as a CEO to triple the profits of his corporation? Did he devote his life to becoming a billionaire?

No, he did not waste his life in that way. Perhaps he accomplished something far more important. He had experienced the tragedy of the Civil War, working as a nurse in the military hospitals of Washington, D.C.

He devoted much of his life to continually improving his *Leaves of Grass*. As a result, he gave us a vision of the incredible worth and potential of every single human being. And when we learn to wed, metaphorically, our everyday concrete and visible behavior to that invisible vision, there is absolutely no limit to how far we all can go toward personal and world development.

...

C. Wright Mills' *The Sociological Imagination* (1959/2000) gave us a vision of how we can open up to an immense range of ideas in our efforts to understand self and world. His mantra was, "Take it big," going along with the fact that he was a tall and wide Texan.

We can extend that imagination to move outside of the academic world and include our interaction with a wide range of people.

An example of the power of such social interaction is illustrated by Frans Johansson in his book, *The Medici Effect*. Johansson, whose father is Swedish and whose mother is African-American/Cherokee, emphasized the importance of diverse interactions for developing innovations. The Medicis, a banking family in Florence during the Renaissance period, funded sculptors, scientists, poets, philosophers, painters and architects who broke down barriers between disciplines and cultures. As a result, the city of Florence became the center of a creative explosion that went on to influence all of Europe and far beyond.

The musical career of Arthur Freed provides a more recent example of the Medici Effect. After initially working as a singer and writer on the vaudeville circuit with the Marx Brothers, he was hired by Metro-Goldwyn-Mayer as an associate producer and later as a producer. Instead of micro-managing the work of his directors and choreographers, he allowed them free rein, resulting in genuine interaction and paralleling the approach of the Medicis. The result was genuine interaction, by contrast with the bureaucratic orientation of micromanagement by committee.

What Freed was able to achieve is most extraordinary. After his efforts in helping to produce *The Wizard of Oz* (1939), he produced a series of Broadway musicals: *Babes in Arms* (1939), *Show Boat* (1951), *Singin' in the Rain* (1952), *An American in Paris* (1951), and *Gigi* (1958). The range of stars he mentored is mind-boggling. It includes Vincente Minnelli, Betty Comden, Adolph Green, Frank Sinatra, Gene Kelly, June Allyson, Red Skelton, Lena Horne, Jane Powell, Esther Williams, Cyd Charisse, Ann Miller, Vera-Ellen, Judy Garland and Fred Astaire.

We have given to academicians a monopoly over the use of the term "scientific method" for their own work. But they suffer as a result by having great difficulty in getting people outside of academia to pay attention to their findings. And people—such as the Medicis, Frans Johansson and Arthur Freed—suffer from a lack of academic credibility attached to their own highly successful achievements.

But the time is long past due when they all should be seen as making use of that method, defined broadly to include both interactions with ideas and with people.

...

Tom tells this story he recalls when he worked as a sheriff's deputy:

> An evangelical church, which enjoyed what some of us outsiders described as a "Jumping for Jesus" celebration, had just completed a hand-clapping hymn of joy, when, in an ecstatic moment, George Dunkins collapsed back into his pew because he was having a heart attack. The church members were determined to bring him back to complete health through the power of prayer.
>
> After twenty-five minutes and no response from Mr. Dunkins, a nervous usher had called 911, and within minutes an ambulance had arrived. Ten minutes later the EMTs called the Sheriff's Department requesting help. You see, many members were determined to continue with the prayer service. Mrs. Dunkins had actually wrapped her legs around the end of a pew and her arms around the legs of the EMTs gurney. Mr. Dunkins may have fallen down, but sure as hell he wasn't going up to no hospital.
>
> That was the scene I saw when I arrived. Seeking the wisdom of Solomon, I led the congregation in a rousing chorus of the hymn, *Onward Christian Soldiers.* Then I announced, "Brothers and sisters, our dearly departed soul is now in the arms of his Savior. Only the body will go to the hospital. Praise Jesus." Mrs. Dunkins let go, and the service finally came to an end, as had George.

Here we have once again an example of the power of interaction or the Medici Effect. Tom was able to tune in completely to the goals of the congregation. His ministerial background was responsible for that. He was equally tuned in to the goals of the Sheriff's Department, requiring him to transport the dead man to the hospital. As a result of his interactive abilities, he was able to fulfill both goals.

...

Yet another Tom Savage story, this one about an experience that he had as a child, can help us to carry still further our understanding of the Medici Effect.

> Determined to see that young people were exposed to better music than just country-western or rock and roll, once a year the county school board put

elementary school children on a big yellow bus and sent them off to the local civic auditorium for a concert of classical music. This was such a big deal, that after the performance, the media were all on hand to ask the kids how they had enjoyed the concert. I was interviewed, and when asked what my favorite piece had been, I responded, "The Lone Ranger," knowing nothing about the *William Tell Overture*.

Later, adding to my embarrassment, every Sunday night at my beloved local Baptist church there was a congregational sing where you could call out a request for your favorite hymn. Again, displaying my overall ignorance in the field of music, I asked that we all sing "Bringing in the Sheets," evidently a celebration fit for any local laundry service. Actually, I was referring to the popular gospel hymn that goes, "Waiting for the harvest, and the time of reaping, We shall come rejoicing, bringing in the sheaves."

Your Bernie Phillips had a similar experience as a child. I was asked by a parent what time it was. I was listening to the radio at the time, and I mimicked what I'd just heard. I answered, "Bulova watch time." Children answering the same question in reaction to the *Howdy Doody* TV puppet show automatically responded, "It's Howdy Doody time!"

These stories suggest the importance for parents to take a decisive role in the evolutionary education of their children. Such interaction, exemplifying the Medici Effect, parallels an interdisciplinary approach to knowledge. We have learned that it is the early years of a child's experiences that shape the child's understanding of self and world. And parents who have an evolutionary understanding can move children away from abject conformity to the powers that be and toward a wide variety of experiences.

There is also the importance of the mass media for helping parents educate their children. When television was first invented, there were high hopes that it would play a significant educational role, hopes that were soon dashed. Yet a vision for television that parallels John Dewey's educational vision for all institutions need no longer remain an unfulfilled dream. Parents, backed up by television, need not wait for formal education to teach their children the scientific method. Given their own understanding of that method, they need not rely on the big yellow bus of the county school board to help them with this process. The media are a basic interactive tool in today's world.

A new feature at a library illustrates this idea of learning from people, as is emphasized within oral society, and not just from published materials, as is the focus within literate society. This is an approach described by Carla Seidman, in an article within the *Sarasota Herald-Tribune*.

Seidman was utterly delighted to learn of a new monthly feature introduced by Darla Kuh at the North Sarasota Library. It's called "Check Out a Person." It is modeled after the Human Library (www.humanlibrary.org) with available "titles" that include an alcoholic, a single mother, a soldier with PTSD, a Muslim, a refugee and someone with HIV":

> Kuh has modeled the local program along the same lines. "We're trying to bring together people who might not normally cross paths," she says.
>
> "You're meeting someone you would not meet in your normal daily life, someone outside your normal experiences." (2018: B1)

Here we have a wonderful illustration of how we all can learn to move in an evolutionary direction. Presently, just as Kuh claims, we all follow our "Indian paths" in our movements around town, failing to meet people who might enlarge our perspectives.

…

A story based on Tom's adult experiences can illustrate this extension of the scientific method to what Johansson called the Medici Effect.

A young couple asked him if he would join them in a wedding ceremony, and he agreed, for he was indeed a minister. They wanted the ceremony to take place on a beach. He said that they were in luck, because his current patrol zone—he was also a sheriff's deputy—included the local beach. He would take his dinner break to do the wedding, but then he would have to leave. He warned the couple that the beach is a public space, and curious people might come over to see what was happening. They said, "No problem."

On the appointed day he arrived, got out of his patrol car, put his robe on over his uniform, went down to the beach, and began the service with the traditional words, "Dearly beloved, we are gathered together…" Then he looked up only to see an inebriated person staggering his way toward the wedding party. He continued reading the wedding vows, when the drunk man yelled out, "You're not really going to marry that bitch, are you?"

Well, Tom was not about to get into an argument or debate with a drunk, so his first response was to just ignore him. But in a few minutes, the man yelled out something even more offensive. At that point Tom lowered his book, pointed directly at the drunk man, and said, "You need to shut up and get out of here, or you're going to jail." The drunk said, "What are you going to do…call the cops?" And, like Superman, Tom opened his robe, exposed his uniform, and said, "We don't need to call the cops, dude, we're already here." The drunk took off like gangbusters, and the wedding proceeded with no more trouble.

Tom's evolutionary vision was illustrated by his two careers. How many people have combined occupations that yield such different experiences, namely, over two decades as a minister and over two decades as a sheriff's deputy?

Tom is not alone in his double career, for more and more individuals, given our increased life spans, are pursuing not only double careers but multiple careers. This is illustrated by those who retire from years of military and government service to enter other occupations. Yet Tom did not stop with his two occupations. By joining Andy, Neil, Max, and me in writing this book, he enters a third career as an author.

...

We turn here to a most unusual economist, E. F. Schumacher. His *Small Is Beautiful: Economics As If People Mattered* (1973) opens up for us an understanding of both the limitations of economic institutions and organizations throughout the world as well as a direction for making those institutions more productive.

Schumacher claimed that "One of the most fateful errors of our age is the belief [that] the problem of production has been solved." For him, a genuine solution must satisfy the three objectives that "Buddhist economics" calls for: "to give a man a chance to utilize and develop his faculties; to enable him to overcome his ego-centeredness by joining with other people in a common task; and to bring forth the goods and services needed for a becoming existence."

Schumacher saw existing patterns of production as failing on those first two aims. He joins Marx's early essay on alienation in seeing the individual's isolation as a basic problem. He also joins that essay's view that much of work requires meaningless and boring efforts, and fails to give the worker opportunities to "utilize and develop his faculties."

By contrast with present procedures for production, Schumacher pointed toward the kind of education that can prepare both workers and management for following the three ideals of Buddhist economics. He followed the ideal of a broad liberal arts and sciences education instead of a narrow vocational education centered only on gaining employment.

...

Andy Plotkin notes in his doctoral dissertation that people—everyday people and experts alike—are unaware of their own basic assumptions or choices. Just as Monsieur Jourdain remained unaware that he was speaking prose all his life, so we are all unaware that we are adopting the invisible stance of a bureaucratic way of life.

In an article based on his thesis (2016), Andy discusses the link between people's bureaucratic metaphysical stance and their emphasis on using dichotomous language. He found such language to be most stereotypical, standing in the way of effective communication. Yet by making visible our invisible bureaucratic choices, we can become aware of just how stereotypical our linguistic behavior is. And we can then learn to eliminate such barriers to close communication. We can add a gradational approach to our usage of dichotomies.

How do we actually respond to the great metaphysical questions of life? In a Woody Allen way, we might say that the aim of life is to find a place where you can get a really good hot pastrami sandwich, Nathan's hot dogs notwithstanding. Tom recalls one night at the seminary when three fellow candidates for the ministry rushed into his dorm room and said, "Let's go get a pizza." Tom replied, "I'm sitting here laboring over the question regarding the meaning of life, and you want me to go with you to get pizza?" It was delicious.

Schumacher was much concerned about the devastation of the environment resulting from a materialistic focus on achieving wealth. He was also aware that the consumption of nonrenewable natural resources by the rich passengers of Spaceship Earth yields an unsustainable economy in the long run. By consuming this "capital," which is the basis for production, it is only a matter of time before productive ability reaches a dead-end.

To address the question of how to actually solve the problem of production, let us imagine, for example, the application of our own ideas about applying the power of the scientific method and language to a business organization such as, say, the Ford Motor Company.

I have deliberately selected the Ford Motor Company for a reason. It was Henry Ford who succeeded in empowering his workers by announcing on January 5, 1914, to pay them $5 per day, the equivalent of $120 today. Instead of taking advantage of workers by paying them as little as possible, Ford helped them. He also enabled them to buy the cars that they produced, thus increasing his bottom line.

As a result, he attracted the very best mechanics in Detroit, raising productivity and eliminating the huge costs that occur with the rapid turnover of workers. I have stressed another kind of empowerment of workers. It is the promise of workers' learning to apply an interdisciplinary scientific method to their work and their lives that will yield increasing productivity.

Ford made other moves in a democratic direction, such as changing from a 48-hour work week to a 40-hour week, and instituting profit sharing for employees who had worked at the company for six months or more. At the same time, however, he promoted anti-Semitism through his newspaper, *The Dearborn Independent,* and he vigorously opposed any collective bargaining with unions as long as he could. Granting his enormous achievements, he lacked a consistent approach to the empowerment or overall development of workers.

...

Ford opened up our understanding of the potential for economic organizations to achieve rapid changes in society through ordinary competitive processes. Given that the wealth of a society remains limited, competition will create losers no less than winners when a given company increases its productivity.

However, the scientific and linguistic education we have described can yield increasing development of the worker's creative or productive abilities, and thus yield more wealth. This would not take away form the potential of other organizations to follow that lead. Through normal competitive processes, it would influence other companies to educate their workers in the same way, thus expanding their own wealth.

As a result, more and more individuals and companies would continue to increase productivity, and thus continue to increase wealth. Therefore, there would be more and more winners and fewer and fewer losers. In such a situation of an expanding pie of rewards, capitalistic competition would move society away from an increasing gap between the rich and the poor and toward a more and more egalitarian society. For such education that empowers the individual would be open to all, and people would have the capacity to develop their personal productivity and use it in everyday life.

What would such economic developments mean for the individual? It would give one the kind of economic security that is presently widely lacking among working individuals. Those who continue to develop in this way would be able to work at a wide variety of jobs, including executive positions. In addition, they would be able to command higher salaries, given not only their present expertise but their increasing problem-solving abilities. Further, workers who were learning in this way would be able to become involved in several types of work at the same time, such as teaching others and consulting with organizations.

...

This would also move the work force toward solving the problem of the elimination of jobs by automation. For the increasingly higher-level skills that workers would gain would keep them ahead of the abilities of robots to duplicate their skills. Those increasing skills of workers would then expand markets.

For example, educational markets would continue to increase, just as the abilities of workers to solve problems would improve. People would be moving toward a renaissance-man-and-woman economy, given their widening range of skills.

To look a bit further at the problem of automation, a theologian asked a computer, "Is there a God?" The computer said it does not have enough information to answer the question, but it will hook up with other computers to find out. When the theologian returns to ask, "Is there a God?" the computer responds, "There is now!"

In a confessional mood, Woody Allen tells us that he has never had a positive relationship with machines. In one particular case, he purchased a television set with a seemingly independent mind. Right in the middle of a favorite program, the TV switched channels. In a moment of uncontrollable frustration, he grabbed a baseball bat and smashed the independent-minded TV into tiny pieces.

Now, Mr. Allen is in an apartment building which had modernized to the extent that all elevators had been automated. You simply told the elevator verbally where you wanted to go, and you were taken to the right floor. But the morning after the incident in his apartment, the elevator asked, "Are you the guy that beat up the TV?" Before Mr. Allen could even respond, the knowing elevator began to take him for a shake-and-bake up-and-down ride, finally tossing him out into the lobby.

I can well understand the actions of the Luddites, a group of English textile workers who destroyed their weaving machinery because they felt that the machines would rob them of their jobs.

This fear of automation is quite understandable. The idea that the field of artificial intelligence can yield robots that might one day rebel against their human masters is a frightening one. And if our robots continue to improve their abilities while human beings fail to progress, then this possibility becomes more realistic. However, if we continue to develop, then that fear becomes unreasonable.

Woody Allen reminds us that a too-serious effort to save the world points us away from our emotions and is too focused on pure reason. He writes, "The unexamined life is not worth living. The examined life is no picnic, either." He goes on to write: "I don't want to achieve immortality through my work . . . I want to achieve it through not dying." He also wrote, "It's not that I'm afraid to die. I just don't want to be there when it happens."

As an example of productivity or problem solving, we turn to the 34-28 victory of the New England Patriots over the Atlanta Falcons in Super Bowl 51 that was watched by 111 million viewers on February 5, 2017. This game illustrates our focus on the importance of understanding the use of the scientific method in everyday life and its relation to productivity.

Given that there was extremely little time for quarterback Tom Brady and his teammates to come back from a 28-3 deficit and tie the game 28-28 and thus go into overtime, every single play that the Patriots made was important. Just one slip-up was all that was needed to end the Patriots' chances. If Edelman hadn't made his incredible catch, if the Falcons' quarterback, Matt Ryan, had not been sacked for a loss to move Atlanta out of field goal range, if White of the Patriots had not delivered on all of his catches, if...if...if..., that would have been the end for the Patriots.

In other words, the Patriots' victory was achieved one step at a time, with each step being absolutely essential to that end result. This focus on what happens in one momentary situation after another emphasizes the importance of one's action from one moment to the next. For such repetitive actions yielded a powerful structure pointing the Patriots toward victory. By so doing, the Patriots illustrated what social scientists have been emphasizing over the years: the enormous power of social structures.

...

On a personal note, six years ago I was diagnosed with myelodysplastic syndrome, a blood cancer that leads to leukemia with a projected average of two years of continued life for my particular diagnosis. The treatments approved by the Food and Drug Administration offered only slight improvement along with substantial side effects. Yet I had a relationship with someone working with a non-FDA-approved substance, a homeopathic product. Research had indicated its substantial positive benefits on conditions similar to my own, with no side effects, granting that this research would not have been sufficient for the FDA.

Friends and physicians warned me against taking anything that was not FDA approved. Yet my own knowledge of the scientific method—having published four textbooks on research methods—led me to be quite wary of existing research procedures, which I saw as quite bureaucratic in their basis on narrow specialization with limited integration of knowledge. Also, I was well aware that the FDA was not interested in looking to a very broad interdisciplinary approach that included

Chinese medicine along with the potentials of herbal treatments. I was also aware of the power of pharmaceutical companies to have substantial influence on the FDA.

What did I do? I refused to conform to the dictates of the FDA. And I'm still here.

Personal productivity is depicted in the recent film, *The Imitation Game*, starring Benedict Cumberbartch and Kiera Knightly. In this film, Alan Turing, the inventor of the universal computer, and his colleagues, were tasked to decipher the "Enigma Code," used by the Nazis during World War II to communicate to their forces on land, sea, and air information on where, when, and how to destroy Allied forces. The Enigma Code was a highly secret device that was incredibly difficult to decipher. The way it worked remained invisible to Turing and his colleagues for a long time.

Yet Turing and his colleagues at Bletchley Park, England, finally succeeded in deciphering the Enigma Code with the aid of the computer that Turing invented. The interactive nature of that computer, joined by Turing's relationships with his colleagues, cracked the enormously complex Enigma Code, shortening World War II by some two years. For the computer with its interactive abilities was able to integrate knowledge, just as Mills and Brandeis were able to accomplish. And Turing required those relationships with his colleagues in order to be able to develop the computer that cracked the Enigma Code. Those relationships illustrated the Medici Effect, which works to enhance the productivity of the individual.

...

At this point, readers may note that very few of our references so far have come from women, and are possibly wondering why. Can readers who are male really imagine what it means to be born into the world as a female, given a history of the world where we have learned to revere so very few females for their accomplishments?

Do you remember how hard you worked in learning to drive a car? That was true for women no less than men. Yet it's embarrassing to admit how often we laughed at jokes about women drivers, told of course by male comedians. Facts tell another story, for most accidents are caused by immature, overly aggressive, male teenage drivers.

The time has come for men to stop their adolescent Tarzan chest-pounding, seeing women as mere sex objects and toys for their own ego satisfaction, while at the same time reducing their victims to abuse and humiliation.

It is time for a woman to respond to the call of the Network film's anchorman, Howard Beale. "Go over to the window, open it up, and yell with all your might, 'I'm mad as hell, and I'm not taking it anymore.'"

The #MeToo movement will expose those who have abused women in the past. These women will recognize that their only shame was their silence. Wake up, guys. It's a new world!

Men must learn how much they need women's help for solving the problems that we all face. And some men must learn that women are their equals in every way. The time has finally come when we all must learn, following Lincoln, that "a house divided against itself cannot stand."

Let's admit it. Sexual politics is all about power, and today's modern women are on the march. Those men of high office who bragged about their past conduct have realized that they are not untouchable after all, and have discovered to their sorrow they are not free to touch anyone at any time.

A day of reckoning has dawned. Sexual harassment and misconduct will no longer be tolerated. It's more than the guilty just losing a job. It's being told that their attitude and bad behavior is wrong on all levels.

...

Given our focus on personal and world evolution in this chapter, we join Abraham H. Maslow, an American psychologist who, along with Carl Rogers, was a founder of the field of humanistic psychology. He was interested in the human potential for further development, as illustrated by his book, *The Further Reaches of Human Nature* (1971).

Instead of following clinical psychologists who work with people who have mental problems, Maslow studied people who he believed were highly developed, such as the anthropologist Ruth Benedict and the psychologist Max Wertheimer. Maslow concluded that we all have "peak experiences," such as feeling within a given situation that we have achieved incredible emotional development. He also believed that peak experiences occur more frequently in more highly developed individuals.

Maslow's work on peak experiences supports the idea that we all have much the same potentials for personal development. This idea suggests a direction for human development: helping people have such experiences ever more frequently so that they can develop personality structures that embody personal productivity. For a structure requires not merely behavior just once in a while, but behavior that is repeated over and over again. It is such structures that include the full power of language and the scientific method, enabling people to move ever further up an evolutionary stairway, helping others to join them.

...

As we move into Part Two emphasizing emotions (or heart), we must not leave behind our understanding of the importance of the intellect (or head).

Part 2:

Commitment ("Heart")

Chapter 3

The Problem: Limited Emotional Development

Hans Christian Anderson tells the tale of a vain Emperor who spent most of his money on new clothes. When two swindlers came to town, he was completely taken in by their claims. "We can weave the most beautiful and expensive cloth imaginable," they said. "But this cloth could not be seen by anyone not fit for his job, or who was just plain stupid. To such, the cloth would be invisible."

Later, when the Emperor went to inspect the garment, naturally he saw nothing. But, remembering the weavers' words, he proclaimed it a marvel of beauty. And everyone else agreed, for if the Emperor could see it, it must be so. But when the Emperor went on parade in his supposed new clothes, a small child declared for all now to see that the Emperor, in fact, was stark naked!

Our leaders and experts are also wearing new clothes. Those clothes are woven out of their supposed understanding of the world's problems and ability to find solutions to them. But given the present state of the world, the time is long past due when the rest of us should proclaim that our leaders and experts—our Emperors—in fact are stark naked. This is what we have attempted to state in the foregoing chapters. Ignorance prevails, granting that very limited understanding does in fact exist.

...

As an independent thinker, Tom has always been frustrated with the ancient myths attempting to explain the trials and tribulations of our human condition.

So he has provided us his own story as a metaphor that he hopes will help us to better understand our life experience.

Picture, if you will, a huge auditorium with enough seats for the entire human race.

As we enter this theatre of life, an usher guides us to our seat. We have been born! Now, this business about the identity of the usher will just have to remain a mystery. I'm still not sure if it's your mother or an angel. But the usher is a necessary character for the telling of this story.

Having been seated, your first realization is that the auditorium's lights are not on. You have been taken into an environment rather dark and mysterious.

And, you're late. The curtain on the stage of life is up. The play has already begun. Human history has not waited for your arrival.

Now, based on the words and actions presented on that stage, you have to guess what has gone on before. Your only clue is the knowledge that the action now taking place is a direct result of the immediate past.

With time and a little patience, you achieve your own personal experiences plus a formal education. This allows you to survive, and, for some, to even flourish.

Then, quite unexpectedly, your usher comes back, taps you on the shoulder, and rather brusquely tells you, "O.K. That's it. You have to Get Out!"

Incredulous, you ask, "What do you mean, Get Out?" In response, the usher repeats himself. But you continue to question this command, saying, "And just why, pray tell, do I have to go?"

The usher replies, "You have to go because you are dead. You're dead, and we need this seat for someone else to be born."

And, friend, whether you are an atheist, agnostic or true believer, it makes no difference. For when you're dead, you have to go.

So, you rise. Yet, I dare say, at least for the more reflective among us, we get up in protest against the absurdity of God's supposed gift of life.

To start with, we have arrived late, with very little time for the meaning of our lives to have been either fully explained or totally justified. Now, we are forced to leave before the last act, the final curtain, when supposedly the end of the story resolves all issues.

Who wrote this play, anyway? Is it any wonder we just don't get it? And, not getting it, are we merely expected to endure life?

Is our human glory to be found in enjoying the freedom to improve ourselves in an imperfect world? Is that the challenge of our Maker?

I confess my fear that far too many will be satisfied to remain simply onlookers of what is happening to them and our world. Many more will even miss out on claiming their fifteen minutes of fame.

How sad that most of us remain inconsequential beings among the billions seated around us in that theatre of life.

The rich and the famous, the beautiful and the Nobel Prize winners, the supposed movers and shakers, appear before us on stage, but we are not there.

We applaud their success, but do not recognize they are as ignorant as we, all failing to discover a truly deeper meaning to life before death.

So it is that most never reach their goals, or never really develop a profound sense of purpose.

...

This book is an effort to rise to the occasion, help us enrich our emotions, generate ennobling ideas and lofty goals, and achieve greater happiness, love, self-confidence and passion.

By so doing, we will abandon our pasts of sadness, hate, guilt, shame, fear and boredom.

By now, readers should realize that, despite the above metaphor of the auditorium, your authors are by no means pessimistic about the human situation. Granting that there is much truth in that image, we believe that every single one of us in that audience has unimaginable power to rise up from his or her seat and change self and world.

Yet it is in this chapter that we center on our limited emotional development, by contrast with the next chapter on the deepening of that development. In order to solve a problem, we must first recognize its existence, just as Tom's metaphor of the auditorium alerts us to basic problems of the human condition.

We begin with the heading, "The Invisible Crisis." The visible crisis is illustrated by dangers from war and terrorism with weapons of mass destruction. The invisible entities that social scientists deal with every day include two elements of consciousness: thoughts and feelings, or ideas and emotions..

The second and final section of the chapter has the heading, "Our Fantasy World." If we are indeed blind to forces we cannot see that threaten us, then we are living in a make-believe world. It then becomes essential for us to learn how to open our eyes to those dangers if we ever expect to challenge them.

Our serious pursuit of the answers to life's basic problems should not get in the way of eating that hot pastrami sandwich. When Henny Youngman said, "Take my wife...PLEASE!" we laughed. And when he added, "I got this cat for my wife" and his neighbor said, "Good trade," we laughed all the more.

THE INVISIBLE CRISIS

One of the greatest social scientists who ever lived was born some twenty-five hundred years ago into the family of a minor ruler of one of India's smaller principalities and raised as a prince of the royal house. He was the Buddha, Gautama Siddartha Sakyamuni.

He unearthed a central problem that we humans have with respect to our goals or aspirations. He identified the problem of *dukkha*, or negative feelings linked to the gap between what people want and are actually able to get. This is our aspirations-fulfillment gap or goal-fulfillment gap: the canyon separating what we want in life and actually achieve. The Buddha also discovered how to build a bridge across that divide. But first we must learn just how that abyss developed in the first place.

We claim that he was a great social scientist—perhaps the greatest one who ever lived—because of three things. He uncovered an absolutely fundamental problem that all humans experience to some degree or another. He had a clear direction for how to make progress on or solve that problem. And he made full use of his incredible insight by proceeding to actively apply that knowledge to himself as well as others.

The Buddha's enlightenment came with his understanding of the Four Noble Truths. It is the First Noble Truth, centering on those negative feelings, which we take up in this chapter. We discuss the other three Noble Truths, designed to transform those feelings into positive ones, in the next chapter.

Our invisible crisis is our failure to fulfill desires that are often unrealistic, such as the hunger for increasing wealth and a materialistic way of life. Such narrow desires erase the many worthwhile things we might learn to do with our lives.

We might also recall the lack of realism of the mother whose son died and who wanted him restored to life. That aspiration, deeply rooted in her basic goals in life, drowned out her freedom to create her own destiny.

The failure of an emphasis on materialism to satisfy us is illustrated by Orson Welles' film, *Citizen Kane*. It is about the life of the newspaper tycoon William Randolph Hearst, who manipulated public opinion so as to influence our entry into the Spanish-American War.

Kane, at the end of his life and surrounded by the huge array of his lavish belongings within his monstrous house, uttered "Rosebud" as his very last word. The camera moves to reveal a sled with the word "Rosebud" on it. It is the sled on which the eight-year-old Kane used to play, the only object of genuine significance to him.

Louis Pasteur, the French chemist and bacteriologist, stated in an address in 1854: "Where observation is concerned, chance favors only the prepared mind." When I was reading about the Buddha, I had emphasized the aspirations-fulfillment gap in a just-completed book published with a colleague: *The Invisible Crisis of Contemporary Society* (2007). As a result, I was well prepared for seeing the significance of the First Noble Truth.

The existence of a wide goal-fulfillment gap is a crucial barrier to one's emotional health. For the full range of an individual's goals can remain unfulfilled as a result, such as further education, a higher standard of living, a happy marriage, loving children, good health, happiness, a fulfilling occupation, and a life that makes a difference to society.

...

In modern times, we have experienced a continuing "revolution of rising expectations," or rapidly increasing expectations or aspirations for whatever can be produced by improving scientific technologies. Advertising makes us aware of what is becoming available, stimulating our desires. This leads to expectations for the endless acquisition of things, only some of which we are able to buy. This results in a widening gap between what we want and are actually able to get.

The idea of this rising expectation revolution was developed by Harlan Cleveland, an American with an extraordinary background. He was U.S. Ambassador to NATO, U.S. Assistant Secretary of State, President of the University of Hawaii, a Peace Corps leader, author of twelve books and hundreds of journal and magazine articles, and recipient of the U.S. Presidential Medal of Freedom as well as 22 honorary degrees.

Almost half a century ago, Cleveland pointed in the direction we have taken in this book. If world problems are increasing, then we can learn to manage them. If our personal problems lack solutions, we can figure out these, too.

Perhaps most important, if the revolution of rising expectations has resulted in large gaps between what people desire and are able to fulfill, then they can learn to do something about it.

Although our focus in this book is on the individual, we should note the implications of the revolution of rising expectations for society as a whole. Just as the individual influences society, so it is that the society influences the individual. Indeed, we have in fact been emphasizing the enormous power of our overall way of life to teach each one of us just how limited we are.

Social scientists have used the individual's aspirations-fulfillment gap—the basis for the Buddha's First Noble Truth—to help explain the onset of political revolutions throughout society. From existing studies (Sztompka, 1994; Gurr, 1970; Davies, 1962), Piotr Sztompka concluded that our lack of understanding of the complexities tied to revolutions—such as control of the army— make it impossible to predict their occurrence at this time. However, these studies of revolution yield evidence for the powerful impact of the aspirations-fulfillment gap on human behavior.

...

We have learned some crucial effects stemming from the goal-fulfillment gap over the past 2500 years since the Buddha's time. A key question is whether or not this invisible gap is increasing or decreasing at the present time.

The book that prepared my colleagues and me for the importance of the Buddha's ideas, *The Invisible Crisis of Contemporary Society* (2007), examined the publications of 32 individuals from the social sciences and some other disciplines. Seventeen of them wrote directly or indirectly about our aspirations-fulfillment gap, with sixteen implying that the gap is increasing. In our own view, there is no question but that desires generally are exceeding their fulfillment to an increasing extent.

Emile Durkheim, one of the founders of the discipline of sociology, has enlightened us about the sources of this gap in *Suicide*, a book he published in 1897 at a time when the industrial revolution was gathering speed in Europe:

> From top to bottom of the ladder, greed is aroused without knowing where to find ultimate foothold. Nothing can calm it, since its goal is far beyond all it can attain…The wise man, knowing how to enjoy achieved results without having constantly to replace them with others, finds in them an attachment to life in the hour of difficulty. But the man who has always pinned all his hopes on the future and lived with his eyes fixed upon it, has nothing in the past as a comfort against the present's afflictions. (255-256)

Durkheim's analysis suggests that this gap can even lead to suicide. An actual suicide is portrayed in Joseph Conrad's novel, *Lord Jim* (2000), also a film starring Peter O'Toole. Conrad portrays the power of buried and unresolved negative emotions like guilt to destroy one's life. That guilt derives not from unrealistic aspirations for ever greater wealth. Rather, it is the result of one's failure to fulfill realistic aspirations for following a moral way of life.

Jim was a British seaman who had signed on as first mate of the *Patna*, a ship with hundreds of Muslims making their holy pilgrimage to Mecca. But the *Patna* is caught by a hurricane, takes on water, and threatens to sink. The Captain and the other officers quickly lower themselves into a lifeboat, abandoning the passengers, and urge Jim to join them. As the wind and rain batter Jim, he is torn between duty and fear, and in a moment of weakness he jumps over the railing into the lifeboat, opening the door to guilt that will plague him for the rest of his life.

When Jim and the other officers finally manage to reach port, they are shocked to see the *Patna* moored there, having been towed by a passing vessel. The others quickly disappear, but Jim decides to stay and face a judicial court of inquiry, which strips him of his naval certificate for abandoning ship.

Jim proceeds to wander the Indonesian archipelago, a derelict among other derelicts, helping others whenever he could, even given the title of "lord" by those he had helped, trying to make up for his failure. But he is never able to forgive himself, to get rid of deep feelings that he has betrayed his ideals. He dies by taking a bullet intended for a boy who he was protecting.

We are all Lord Jim. We, too, fail to live up to the standards that society has taught us. Following the ideas of Freud and modern psychotherapists, our repression of negative emotions enables them to continue to haunt us, just as did Jim's feelings of guilt. Rather than raise those emotions to the surface so that we can deal with them in one way or another, we fail to do so.

But this is much easier said than done. For who has taught us the importance of avoiding emotional repression? Where have we learned the power of guilt over us? In what school have we been given instruction about the ability of repressed emotions to destroy our lives?

...

Karen Horney's *The Neurotic Personality of Our Time* (1937) carries forward Freud's analysis of emotions by including social science knowledge. She practiced psychoanalysis in Berlin before settling in New York, where she continued her practice and taught at the New School for Social Research. But her ideas emphasized the importance of culture and not just biology for understanding the origins of neurosis, departing from some of Freud's basic principles, and she was expelled from the New York Psychoanalytic Institute. She writes:

> When we remember that in every neurosis there are contradictory tendencies which the neurotic is unable to reconcile, the question arises as to whether there are not likewise certain definite contradictions in our culture, which underlie the typical neurotic conflicts...
>
> The second contradiction is that between the stimulation of our needs and our factual frustrations in satisfying them. For economic reasons, needs are constantly being stimulated in our culture by such means as advertisements, "conspicuous consumption," and the ideal of "keeping up with the Joneses." For the great majority, however, the actual fulfillment of these needs is closely restricted. The psychic consequence for the

individual is a constant discrepancy between his desires and their fulfillment. (287–288)

The implications of this "second contradiction" once again return us to the Buddha's First Noble Truth, which remains unrecognized throughout our contemporary scientific world. It is nothing less than "neurosis"—an idea now out of fashion among psychotherapists—that can result from a continuing aspirations-fulfillment gap.

...

Georg Simmel, a founder of the discipline of sociology, was much concerned with the emotional problems created by the dramatic changes throughout Europe from a feudal, rural and agricultural society to a factory-based industrial and urban society.

These basic and rapid changes in people's lives wreaked havoc on the fulfillment of their expectations, yielding that same wide gap between desire and achievement.

Imagine having one's farm suddenly taken over by the construction of a factory on it. Granting that the farmer involved may succeed in becoming a laborer in that factory, his entire pattern of existence has been destroyed.

Let us recall Marx's analysis of the alienation of the factory worker to examine the impact of Europe's rapid process of industrialization. The worker becomes isolated or alienated from the four structures that have to do with his entire way of life: physical, personality, biological and social. The falling off from the fulfillment of the expectations one had in one's former way of life is dramatic.

In his most well-known essay, "The Metropolis and Mental Life," Simmel wrote:

> The deepest problems of modern life flow from the attempt of the individual to maintain the independence and individuality of his existence against the sovereign powers of society, against the weight of the historical heritage and the external culture and technique of life. (1903/1971:324)

What we have here, once again, is reference to the huge problems faced by the individual as industrialization proceeded. These are "the deepest problems" faced by the individual, for his very "independence and individuality" is at stake. The gap here has to do with one's very survival as a unique individual within an industrial economy.

As for one's emotional life in particular, Simmel claimed that metropolitan people learn to intensify their intellect or consciousness at the expense of their emotions in order to deal with "the fluctuations and discontinuities" of city life. This one-sided intellectual orientation is accompanied by very short-term relationships with merchants and other city-dwellers who are rushing about in a losing attempt to fulfill their many goals.

Yet he argues that long-term relationships are those that yield the basis for the emotional expression and emotional development we all require. Those extended and close relations that existed in farming communities were easily lost in the rapid change from farm to metropolis. Once again, we see a failure to achieve what one has learned to expect throughout one's life. The city dweller, who imagines that he or she has somehow become more civilized, has come to lose a fundamental element of life.

The era at the end of the 19th century and the very beginning of the twentieth century in which Simmel was writing still reflected optimism. For democratic institutions had begun to flourish in Europe and the United States. For example, we had Laurence Gronlund's *The Cooperative Commonwealth* (1884), August Bebel's *Woman in the Past, Present, and Future* (1886), Edward Bellamy's *Looking Backward: 2000-1887,* (1888), and H. G. Wells' *A Modern Utopia* (1905).

All of the themes of optimism championed in our book would have resonated with those widespread ideals at that time. Yet those visions fell into the mud of blood-stained trenches in Belgium and France during and immediately after the First World War.

The Great War created a culture of pessimism, replacing the optimism of earlier times.

World War One was for the twentieth century what the Black Death had been for the Middle Ages. Try to imagine confidence in human reason losing its credibility. Perhaps the greater tragedy was a war that lacked any ultimate sense of meaning or purpose.

The devastation of this conflict continued largely because no one wanted to admit defeat. As the machine guns slaughtered the troops, a cynicism and despair took over the battlefield. With almost ten million killed, with thirty million wounded, an entire generation had been slaughtered and maimed.

On the battlefields of World War One liberalism's belief in reason, respect for the worth of the individual, and belief in rational progress, had all been slaughtered and maimed as well. In the end, many veterans lost respect for their governments as well as the political process.

Along with this pessimism about progress of any kind, how can we ignore the emotional impact of this new reality? How can we possibly empathize with the tragedies of mothers and fathers who had lost their sons? Wives who had lost their husbands? Children who had lost their fathers?

If ever there was an event that created a huge gap between what people expected out of life and what they were in fact able to receive, it was the Great War.

All of that pessimism was heightened by the worldwide flu epidemic of 1918, which killed 50 to 100 million people, 3 to 5 percent of the world's population, yielding disillusionment with scientific and medical institutions. Not far behind was the Spanish Civil War, the rise of Nazi Germany, World War II, and the Holocaust.

...

Given the contemporary battle for the American mind, men filled with supposedly good reasons for a new war should bow their heads in shame when confronted with the anguished emotions of a son and his mother in the musical, *1776*, which celebrates the founding of our country.

Early in the war, a small skirmish has taken the lives of a few boys. Others lie bleeding as their mothers rush to the scene to find missing sons. One wounded lad is calling out, "Hey, hey, mama, look sharp."

Try to imagine that mother reaching her son, only to find him mortally wounded.

Try to imagine a son asking his own mother if he is dying, and she must answer, "Yes."

Try to imagine her being forced to bury her son, her child, who will never again cry out, "Hey, hey, mama, look sharp."

Try to imagine the empty days and years that she will suffer without her son. Would that tears could mend a broken heart.

Would that prayer could restore what one has lost.

Would that actions could change what cannot be changed. Would that the lessons of conflict could stop the tragedy of war.

For Death comes as a thief in the night to steal from us those whom we love. And the loss is forever.

If you cannot respond emotionally to this scene, then part of you is already dead.

If you cannot feel the anguish of a boy who is rapidly losing his chance to live out his life, while his life blood drains out of him, then part of you is already dead.

If you cannot understand the trauma experienced in the loss of a loved one, then part of you is already dead.

By not rising up to stand for something, part of you is already dead.

By not going to the window to shout, "War. Hell no! We're not going to accept it anymore," then you are dead.

Remember, the only just war should be against disease, ignorance and poverty. Hey, hey, dear reader, look sharp!

...

On a lighter note that illustrates this same theme of the Buddha's First Noble Truth, there is Tom Savage's story of his experience at a summer camp:

> "Are you up to the challenge?" These were the opening words from the director of Camp Thunderhead, a summer retreat for teenage boys. And what was this challenge for those dreaming of someday becoming big, bad, tough Marines? You had to get up each morning before breakfast, and jump into the camp's unheated swimming pool. And, at five thousand feet those spring-fed mountain waters were cold!

> Out of twenty-four, only three of us completed the task. The reward: A promised silver ring. There we proudly stood at the final campfire, expectantly awaiting our prize.

> The director came up behind us with a silver triangle, striking it three times: ding, ding, ding. That was the silver ring. The next sound was a large splash, as we threw the director into the pool. Tragically, he did not drown, and survived to ask the next group of campers, "Are you up to the challenge?"

The camp director left his campers totally deceived, desperately wanting something that they would never get. Here we have another illustration of treating the individual as insignificant. Yet isn't this a very common experience that we all have in contemporary society? Don't we all develop desires to be rich, to be famous, to have a high IQ, to have lots of close friends, to travel around the world, to be handsome or beautiful, to win the Nobel Prize, to live a truly meaningful life, to change the world? Does not the campers' disappointment simply parallel all of our experiences of wanting something the world is not prepared to give.

...

Another experience Tom had, this time with one of his parishioners, can strengthen the idea that our way of life continues to yield that same very wide gap between desire and fulfillment.

> A senior citizen in my congregation was found to be writing checks for five, ten, twenty, even fifty thousand dollars, when he had absolutely no money in the bank to back them up. When confronted, with great annoyance he said, "Where's the crime? The money is not for me. It's for charity!"

Is this not like Washington politicians who create programs servicing the general public, and, however beneficial, are not backed by any adequate funding proposals to pay for these programs? The result is the pain and suffering people feel when their expectations are raised by political promises only to be dashed by what happens afterwards.

Just as Tom's parishioner had no way of backing up his charitable donations with actual cash, and the same for Washington politicians and their planned beneficial programs, this is the general situation for the rest of us. Our outward orientation works against our being realistic about our actual ability to fulfill our aspirations. We want to be praised for our good intentions, just as the parishioner desired.

However, those Washington politicians and the rest of us can be called out for our unrealistic aspirations, just as the little boy in Hans Christian Anderson's tale cries out, "Look! The Emperor has no clothes." It is then that we are shown to have our heads in the clouds and our feet off in space. However, it is far better for us not to depend on others to recognize our lack of realism, but to depend on ourselves.

OUR FANTASY WORLD

Let us return to our discussion of how advertising takes away our love of ourselves and offers it back for the price of the product, granting that we can never buy that love back because far too many products are involved.

Let us also gain awareness of just how ubiquitous advertising is in the modern world, for it haunts us wherever we go and in all hours of the day and night.

Let us now question how it is possible for advertising to remain credible. For its claims are far from scientific ones, yet corporations would not continue to spend billions on advertising unless it actually works for them.

John Berger's conclusion in his *Ways of Seeing* (1985) was this:

> It remains credible because the truthfulness of publicity is judged, not by the real fulfillment of its promises, but by the relevance of its fantasies to those of the spectator-buyer. Its essential application is not to reality but to daydreams. (149)

If Berger is correct, and we believe he is, then we can begin to understand why we are presently living in an era when scientific facts, and other facts of all kinds, are attacked as "fake news," and not just in the United States.

Given that advertising has succeeded in creating a fantasy world that so many of us dwell in, it has prepared us for our present era.

But it is unfair to place all of the blame for our lack of realism on advertising. We have depended on our educational system to teach more and more of us to value truth. Apparently, we were wrong.

...

The historian Daniel Boorstin illustrates our lack of realism in his *The Image*:

> In this book I describe the world of our making, how we have used our wealth, our literacy, our technology, and our progress, to create the thicket of unreality which stands between us and the facts of life…[E]ach of us individually provides the market and the demand which flood our experience. We want and we believe these illusions because we suffer from extravagant expectations. We expect too much of the world…

> We expect the contradictory and the impossible. We expect compact cars which are spacious; luxurious cars which are economical. We expect to be rich and charitable, powerful and merciful, active and reflective, kind and competitive. We expect to be inspired by mediocre appeals for "excellence," …to eat and stay thin, to be constantly on the move and ever more neighborly…to revere God and to be God. Never…have a people felt more deceived and disappointed. For never has a people expected so much more than the world could offer. (1961: 3-4, 6)

Within the many fields of education, the social sciences—sociology, psychology, anthropology, history, economics and political science—should bear much of the blame for our present situation. There is indeed growing awareness among social scientists that they should enter the public arena of the mass media and contribute to our understanding of human behavior and human problems. As yet, however, very little of this nature has occurred.

Our escape from reality really goes very far back in history. Let us not forget the Buddha's First Noble Truth. That escape has been a central problem of the human race throughout our history.

Yet many of us believed that with the Enlightenment era of the eighteenth century, with the continuing development of the sciences, with the further development of mass education, and most recently with the rise of the internet, that ignorance was being banished to an increasing degree.

Apparently, we were wrong, or at least wrong to a great extent.

…

Our widespread lack of ability to pay attention to reality has much in common with a childlike view of the world. Tom Savage tells of his reaction to the story of "The Three Little Pigs" and the big, bad wolf when he was five years old:

> What had the pigs done? Built three little houses: one of straw, one of sticks, and one of bricks. I knew what was going to happen even before my mother finished reading the story to me. But I couldn't wait to see if my guess had been right.
>
> I wasn't prepared for the wolf coming down the chimney and ending up in a pot of boiling water. That seemed a bit excessive, especially to someone who was later concerned about the fate of the Pharaoh's horses when they crossed the Red Sea in pursuit of the Jews and were met with the closing of the Red Sea's waters.
>
> No. The three little pigs should have warned the wolf he could get hurt trying to enter their residence. I guess I felt at that tender age that even wolves had rights, even if they were bad. Maybe the wolf could have been sent to a place where bad wolves were made good.
>
> In the best of all possible worlds, bad wolves can be made good, prisoners can be reformed so that they don't return to prison, the Pharaoh's horses can swim ashore, war and terrorism can be eliminated, the world can prevent climate change from happening, poor nations can become richer and poor individuals can move toward a decent standard of living, there can be free higher education for all, increasing costs of medical care can be contained and medical expenses for the entire population can be afforded, disease can be conquered to an increasing extent, work can become ever

more meaningful, the rate of divorces can be reversed, education at every level can continue to be improved, the arts can prosper, and all of us can continue to develop intellectually, emotionally, and in our problem-solving ability with no limit.

Tom's ideas appear to be ridiculous to us adults, who are supposedly educated to face reality. But are we in fact able to take facts into account to the extent that we claim? The ideas of the sociologists Arthur J. Vidich and Joseph Bensman can help us here, for they build on profound insights from none other than Sigmund Freud. It was Freud who spread widespread awareness of the existence of the unconscious within each of us, an idea that parallels our own emphasis on invisible forces that shape our lives.

We might also see Vidich and Bensman as building on the ideas of another great psychoanalyst, Carl Jung. He saw the most important human project as making visible the invisible forces shaping human behavior in his The Undiscovered Self (1957/2006).

Let us also recall that almost all of the basic concepts of social scientists cannot be seen, ideas such as "bureaucracy," "alienation," "self-image," "social stratification" (persisting hierarchy, that is), "values," "the scientific method," and "culture."

By contrast with the idea of invisibility, let us not forget the theme of Part One of this book: "Vision." Recall that ancient biblical proverb: "Without a vision the people perish." To the extent that invisible forces dominate our lives, it remains most difficult for us to develop a vision that furthers our potential for personal and world development. Are we then fated to remain in "the country of the blind"?

Vidich and Bensman collaborated on a study in the late 1950s of "Springdale," a town in upper New York State, publishing their results as Small Town in Mass Society: Class, Power and Religion in a Rural Community (1960).

Springdale Township had a population of only about 3,000 when they did their study. Economically, the central village—with a population of about 1,000—served as a farm trading center, with retail establishments selling farm merchandise, and with the presence of a milk collecting plant. Lumber was the chief economic resource of the community, with a commercial sawmill operated by two families.

The two researchers saw their study as "an attempt to explore the foundations of social life in a community which lacks the power to control the institutions that regulate and determine its existence" (1960: x).

More specifically, they explored the divergence between the way the community saw itself, on the one hand, and the actual realities of their existence, on the other hand:

> (1) The small-town resident assumes the role of the warm, friendly, sociable, helpful good neighbor and friend. However, the forms of social competition and the struggle for individual success...[tend] to devalue his neighbors' success...

(2) The goal of success as a major value and meaning in life stands in contrast to the inaccessibility of the means to achieving success...[which] are not equally available to all groups...

(3) The illusion of democratic control over his own affairs given by the formal structure of government stands in sharp contrast to the actual basis of local politics...Most of the professionals, the old aristocrats, workers, traditional farmers and all of the shack people stand entirely outside the decision making process...

(4) The belief and illusion of local independence and self-determination prevent a recognition of the central place of national and state institutions in local affairs. The reality of outside institutional dominance...is given only subliminal, pragmatic recognition... (1960)

Vidich and Bensman's explanation of how individuals managed to adjust to the lack of reality of the Springdalers has implications for the rest of us. How do we manage to adjust to our own life in a fantasy world? Here are three ways that they and we cope:

(1) The Technique of Particularization:

All these explicit mentions of community dependence are made in the context of highly specific detailed cases. No generalization sums up these detailed statements, so that individuals are not explicitly aware of the total amount of their dependence. Particularizations prevent the realization of the total impression...The technique of particularization is one of the most pervasive ways of avoiding reality. The Springdaler is able to maintain his equalitarian ideology because he avoids generalizing about class differences. The attributes of class are seen only in terms of the particular behavior of particular persons.... (1960: 299)

2) The Falsification of Memory:

The realization of lack of fulfillment of aspiration and ambition might pose an unsolvable personal problem if the falsification of memory did not occur, and if the hopes and ambitions of a past decade or two remained salient in the present perspective. But the individual, as he passes through time, does not live in spans of decades or years. Rather, he lives in terms of seasons, days and hours and the focus of his attention is turned to immediate pressures, pleasures and events...As a consequence, his present self, instead of entertaining the youthful dream of a 500–acre farm, entertains the plan to buy a home freezer by the fall...(1960: 303)

(3) The Externalization of the Self:

The greatest dangers to a system of illusions which is threatened by an uncompromising reality are introspection and thought...The major technique of self-avoidance is work...Religious activities such as suppers,

choirs and fund raising involve a great deal of physical and social effort and support the process of continuous externalization....

But the people of Springdale are unwilling to recognize the defeat of their values, their personal impotence in the face of larger events and any failure in their way of life. By techniques of self-avoidance and self-deception, they strive to avoid facing issues which, if recognized, would threaten the total fabric of their personal and social existence....

Because they do not recognize their defeat, they are not defeated. The compromises, the self-deception and the self-avoidance are mechanisms which work; for, in operating on the basis of contradictory, illogical and conflicting assumptions, they are able to cope in their day-to-day lives with their immediate problems in a way that permits some degree of satisfaction, recognition and achievement. (1960: 311–320)

Vidich and Bensman succeed in giving us an understanding of just how the Springdalers, and the rest of us, manage to live in our world of unreality with these three powerful procedures.

"The Technique of Particularization" exemplifies our bureaucratic emphasis on narrow specialization without the integration of knowledge. Just as the Springdalers avoid facing the reality of a hierarchy among their social classes, so do narrow specialists throughout the academic world avoid facing the reality of their failure to follow the scientific requirement of standing on the shoulders of giants.

"The Falsification of Memory" of the Springdalers is once again paralleled throughout the social sciences with their ahistorical orientation. Lip service is given to such founders of sociology as Marx, Durkheim, Weber and Simmel without genuinely building on their profound and broad ideas.

As for "The Externalization of Self," here we have a partial answer for the avoidance of developing a vision of the potentials of the individual by social scientists and society. For any focus on the individual would threaten one's conformity to our bureaucratic way of life. Without any alternative to our present pattern of behavior, we would be cutting the ground out from under us with nowhere else to stand.

We do not quarrel with Vidich and Bensman's conclusion that the avoidance of reality by the Springdalers "permits some degree of satisfaction, recognition and achievement." However, that avoidance prevents them from both moving toward more meaningful personal lives as well as gaining the ability to help solve world problems.

Moving further toward the present, here is a story told to me by Tom Savage, who had visited Saigon in the late 1970s after the Vietnam War:

Onto the downtown public square came an elderly man pushing a handcart piled high with small wooden cages stuffed with birds that can hardly move. Over his cart flies a banner with English words, "Free the Birds. 5¢." Tom could not resist giving the old man a five dollar bill, commanding him to free all the birds, which he did.

Up they flew, flapping and squawking, rejoicing in their new-found freedom, circling the public square before flying back to the pens where they were fed. The old man then went back up to the pens, re-stuffed the birds into their cages, and placed them on his handcart, Returning to the street, he looked for the next gullible tourist who would free the birds for 5¢.

Those gullible tourists were following Einstein's definition of insanity: using the same procedures over and over again, but expecting a different result. Just as they continue to try to free the birds over and over again only to discover them once again in cages, so are they using the same procedures to free the birds, yet a different result is not forthcoming.

We might apply such insane behavior to the American administration's efforts to win the war in Vietnam, not having learned from the French who failed before them. The U.S. sprayed the country with ever more Agent Orange, achieved the deaths of ever more human beings on both sides, expected a different result from the same procedures, yet actually achieved the same negative results from its insanity.

...

Ending this chapter with more contemporary research bearing on our emotional problems, let us consider an analysis of sex on the American college campus, primarily in residential rather than commuter campuses. The sociologist Lisa Wade's *American Hookup: The New Culture of Sex on Campus* (2017) describes the attempts by college students to divorce sexual relationships from any deep emotional attachment. For this divorce permits freedom to engage in "hookups" that supposedly have no implications for romantic relationships.

The type of sex that Wade describes, often following heavy drinking, varies from only kissing and touching to oral sex and intercourse. But the norms for hookups require that the students avoid "catching feelings" (46). If feelings arise, they should be hidden. Such emotional repression is by no means completely effective, as many long-term relationships develop that begin with hookups.

Here once again we have the flight from reality that is characteristic of our way of life. Just as in the case of the Springdalers, we cannot question in any serious way that kind of life without an alternative.

After seven years of research and writing which has built on what we've done throughout our professional lives, your authors are convinced that we have indeed emerged with an alternative that permits far more than "satisfaction, recognition and achievement." For humans have no more than just begun our evolutionary journey.

In future times all of our achievements will appear to future generations much like we presently view accomplishments during the Middle Ages or even earlier times.

Given the problems that we all face today, it is indeed difficult to move beyond the pessimism that we see all around us. Yet your authors are here to accentuate the positive, and to ground that optimism on solid knowledge from the academic world coupled with our own personal experiences.

Yes, it is true that we are living in the midst of an invisible crisis. Yes, it is also the case that we are located in a fantasy world.

But it is equally true that there are tools, such as language and the scientific method, that can enable us to see what we were unable to see. Those tools can in turn give us the motivation we require to move from pessimism toward optimism, from despair toward joy, from fear toward confidence, based on new-found abilities to create self and world.

CHAPTER 4

The Solution: Deepening Emotional Development

THE EASTERN STRATEGY

Gautama, later known as the Buddha, was unusual as a founder of a great movement, for his background was neither simple nor common. He was a prince, surrounded by all the opulence and luxury of that station. Yet, despite his wealth, he found himself feeling incomplete, with life at times quite meaningless and empty. What, he wondered, was life all about beyond the walls of the palace?

Now, we smile today at the early myth stories attributed to the lives of famous persons. For the Buddha, a tale is told of how he left his palace home to experience a larger world, and he encountered "four sights," four realities of the human condition that wealth supposedly protected one from seeing or experiencing.

The first sight was a person who was ill, sick more in body than mind. The second sight was of an elderly person, bent over with the cares of time and physical decline. The third sight was of a funeral. Here was the end of life for all who had ever lived. The fourth sight was of a wandering monk who was trying to understand the meaning and significance of the first three sights.

Gautama knew what he must do: Go on his own journey of self-discovery. In an act of total renunciation of his past, he left the palace and its pleasures, left his wife and child, and began his pilgrimage, hoping to bring answers to life's mysteries.

Now, Hinduism was the basic religion and faith of the land, with meditation and contemplation being the paths for enlightenment. Gautama had abandoned the distraction of material comforts. He even reduced his reliance on the necessities of food and water to the extent that he had become quite emaciated. Surely this was not the right way to enlightenment, for if he continued on this path he would die.

Material goods in abundance, too, had left him feeling lost. This also was a false path. There must be a Middle Way, and this realization became the Buddha's enlightenment.

A follower had once asked the Buddha, "Are you a God?" "No," responded the Buddha, "I am not a God."

"Are you, then, a prophet?"

"No, said the Buddha, "I am not a prophet.

Finally, in total frustration, the follower blurted out, "Then, what are you?"

"I am Awake," replied the Buddha. And to be awake is to be aware. We hear this echoed in the Christian hymn, Amazing Grace, "I once was lost, but now am found, once blind, but now I see." This awareness makes all the difference.

Now enlightened, the Buddha put forward Four Noble Truths:

First – all of life entails frustration. The Buddha called this reality "dukkha," based on our failure to fulfill our wants or aspirations.

Second – following the idea that is the basis for the sciences, along with a rational understanding of the world, every effect or occurrence has a cause or causes.

Third – we should understand that by removing our unrealistic desires, such as for a materialistic life of total luxury, and by limiting our desires to what we can actually achieve, we can eliminate our frustration and fulfill those desires. By removing the cause of a problem, we remove the problem.

Fourth – we can accomplish this by following an Eightfold Path of appropriate thoughts, goals, and actions.

The Buddha traveled throughout India, teaching others how to achieve the Enlightenment that he had gained. That teaching proved to be so meaningful, so important and so effective that Buddhism became a world religion.

Yet we need not become Buddhists to learn from and become empowered by the Buddha's Four Noble Truths and Eightfold Noble Path. Granting that we have been thrown into a much different kind of world than that experienced by the Buddha, those truths and that path can relieve our own suffering.

For now as then, we experience the pain of unrealistic desires or wants. Now as then, every effect has causes.

Now as then, we can understand that becoming more realistic in our desires will relieve our suffering.

Now as then, we can do this with the right kind of thoughts, goals, and actions.

…

Tom Savage's personal experience in Nepal, described as follows, can deepen our understanding:

My major professor at the Boston University School of Theology had given me a letter of introduction for visiting a Buddhist monastery in Nepal. I had been advised to arrive at 6 a.m. The monks had left at 5 a.m. with their begging bowls. I arrived promptly on time as instructed at 6 a.m., and no one was there to greet me.

As time wore on, I began to go through a variety of emotional states: frustration, exasperation, and by 9 o'clock anger at such rudeness. At 9:30, emotionally exhausted, I had fully accepted my situation. Then, suddenly the door to the monastery parted and a saffron-robed monk said in perfect English, 'Now that you are open, you may come in.'

I had been put through a Buddhist exercise that clears the mind of trivial thoughts in preparation for possible Enlightenment.

Tom's Western orientation operated on him almost all the time that he was waiting to be greeted. For all he was able to think of was the rudeness of the monk who had told him to arrive at 6 a.m. He was on time, even early. Where were they?

Waiting with frustration, he had been unable to focus on any other things he might have done, such as thinking about his own life, about the nature of Buddhism, about what he hoped to learn at the monastery, about one of his courses at his School of Theology, or about anything else whatsoever. He might even have used all of that waiting time to engage in an exercise like walking around the temple grounds. He might even have questioned his own Western sense of time as well as his own negative emotional state.

But no, his Western outward orientation took him away from such inward behavior. He had been forced to clear his mind of all such trivia. Only a cleared mind is open to hear a new voice.

His Western emotions illustrated growing frustration. And the combination of that frustration with his outward orientation was a formula for the anger that he came to direct at the monk who had told him when to arrive.

However, as time continued to pass, those negative emotions finally departed, for he finally "had fully accepted" his situation. Not everyone would have achieved that clearing of the mind and the emotions, but Tom was able to accomplish that.

Perhaps he finally realized what was happening. For he had studied Buddhism in his classes on comparative religions. He understood intellectually the difference between an Eastern inward orientation and a Western outward perspective.

But an intellectual understanding had not proved to be enough. He had to actually experience that Buddhist exercise, and not just study it, in order to finally become open to Enlightenment.

We might contrast Tom's first reaction to that long period of waiting with that of the monk. Granting that the appointed hour had passed, the monk was not oriented to the outward passage of time but to Tom's inward state of mind. For the monk, the passage of time enabled Tom to open up inwardly to the possibility of Enlightenment. That very inward orientation had helped the Buddha develop his Noble Truths.

As a result of his experience in Nepal, Tom learned about the depth and breadth of our Western orientation, which even reaches out to a sense of time. Changing that orientation cannot be achieved simply by study. Following President Theodore Roosevelt's mantra, "The credit belongs to the man who is actually in the arena," just as Tom had actually entered the Buddhist monastery in Nepal.

What Tom had achieved as a result of his experience in that monastery was not only an awareness of the difficulties involved in narrowing his Western gap between expectations for timely service and their fulfillment. He was able to succeed in conquering that problem and learned something far more important than subservience to the clock. That was his inner emotional openness to learning.

Yet can we in the West learn from Tom's experience?

Can we somehow move beyond our materialistic experiences of shopping till we drop and turn toward a more significant and satisfying way of life?

Can we learn to escape from our fantasy world into a pattern of behavior that is increasingly more realistic?

Given current world problems, can ordinary individuals help to make progress on them by closing their gap between desires and achievements?

Beyond our experiences of emotional repression, can we learn to move toward emotional expression?

Can we learn, as Tom did, "to enter the arena" of personal experience and emerge with a direction that follows the Buddha's "Eastern strategy" for confronting emotional problems?

Is it possible for us in the West to pay attention to the ideas of historical figures like Socrates and examine our own lives so as to take facts into account?

Would it be helpful for us to learn how to make fuller usage of the scientific method and language in our efforts to live a more meaningful life?

Is there a way of life that can take us beyond "some degree of satisfaction, recognition and achievement" so as to emphasize the Eastern emphasis on feelings no less than the Western focus on facts?

Do our experiences in the Western world give us a positive direction to add to the Buddha's Eastern strategy, despite the limitations of our outward orientation?

THE EAST-WEST STRATEGY

Andy Plotkin's artist mother, Edna Hibel, pointed us toward an East-West strategy for living a fuller life when she wrote, "I couldn't paint what I painted yesterday because I've changed" (1974: 122). She added to this idea as follows:

> You learn all the technical things to help you be yourself. You know, 'To thine own self be true—.' It sounds simple to be yourself, but, oh my, it's a struggle. But the better I learn to handle my tools and the more self-confident I become, the easier it is to be myself. (104)

Hibel was writing not just about the artist but about the rest of us as well. Within our present way of life it is indeed difficult "to be yourself," to follow Shakespeare's advice, "To thine own self be true," to conquer one's own orientation toward conformity. Yet it is possible to emerge from that struggle with increasing self-confidence and go on to follow the kaizen idea of continuing improvement throughout one's everyday life.

The poet Robert Browning suggested this idea when he wrote, "Ah, but a man's reach should exceed his grasp, Or what's a heaven for?" For your authors, that "heaven" is no limit to one's continuing improvement throughout one's entire life.

...

Western history, despite our overall outward orientation, has succeeded in pointing to an extent in an East-West direction, as illustrated by my own previous assessment:

> History's movement toward democratic ideals suggests nothing less than the increasing importance and potential of every single individual. For example, we have the 18th-century American and French revolutions. And we have our more recent social movements that carry still further our democratic ideals: the American civil rights movement, women's movement, gay, lesbian and transgender movement, senior movement, and disability movement.

> Two social scientists, S. M. Miller and Anthony J. Savoie, have called these movements the "respect revolution" of the Twentieth Century (2002: 8-12). They trace this revolution as including a number of crucial events: the 1954 Supreme Court decision in *Brown v. the Board of Education of Topeka, Kansas*, the burial of using the term "girls" for women, the resistance to the attack by police on the Stonewall gay bar…the passage of the Americans with Disabilities Act, the passage of the Older Americans Act. (Phillips, 2012: 79-80)

The "respect revolution" is a direct attack on conformity to persisting hierarchy, behavior that is central to our bureaucratic way of life. This is an idea that has been advanced by Robert W. Fuller, former President of Oberlin College. He has developed the concept of "rankism" to yield further insight into what Miller and Savoie mean by their concept of respect:

> Rankism insults the dignity of subordinates by treating them as invisible nobodies…Nobodies are insulted, disrespected exploited, ignored…It might be supposed that if one overcame tendencies to racism, sexism, ageism, and other narrowly defined forms of discrimination, one would be purged of rankism as well. But rankism is not just another ism. It subsumes the familiar dishonorable isms. It's the mother of them all. (2003, 5)

Following Fuller's approach in his book, *Somebodies and Nobodies: Overcoming the Abuse of Rank*, "rankism" includes such forms of showing disrespect as "heightism," "weightism," "beautyism," and any form of disrespect whatsoever. Fuller has succeeded in initiating a new social movement focusing on rankism, and he develops further insight about this movement in a later book, *All Rise: Somebodies, Nobodies, and the Politics of Dignity* (2006).

…

Another story about Tom's experiences can help us to understand more fully how the respect revolution, together with efforts to eliminate rankism, can continue to proceed.

While working during the summer at a Y.M.C.A. Youth Camp, he boarded a school bus completely filled with black children. He found himself thinking: "Man, you done got on the wrong bus."

At the end of the summer, again boarding the same bus, he no longer saw a sea of black, but individuals, most of whom he had come to love, and, yes, a few he wanted to strangle. It took the entire summer for him to get to know these children, and it was the continuing interactions with those children that changed his initial feelings, perhaps from uncertainty and fear to genuine appreciation and love.

Tom illustrated the results of a major theory in social psychology: intergroup contact theory, which centers on the impact of contact between majority and minority group members on the reduction of majority group prejudice. Early studies during World War II illustrated this when soldiers were clustered together in the front lines, where their status was much the same.

These studies have been updated in recent years. For example, an analysis of 515 studies with more than 250,000 subjects has revealed that intergroup contact typically reduces prejudice (Pettigrew and Tropp, 2006).

...

Our focus on the East-West strategy and emotional development should include attention to "values," which may be defined as goals, interests, or ideals that are widely shared within a given community or society. Values are more long-term phenomena than emotions. An example of the importance of values is the idea of "value neutrality."

A basic idea within the academic world that has worked to suppress the emotions of academics is this idea of "value neutrality." Researchers are advised not to let their own values affect the research process in order to avoid biasing the conclusions.

But it appears that this concept of value neutrality has negative consequences. The conclusions of a recent collection of the work of eleven contemporary philosophers of science, *Value-Free Science? Ideals and Illusions* (2007), edited by Harold Kincaid, indicate that arguments for value neutrality are misleading at best, and may well be destructive.

Kincaid concludes that all of us, scientists included, have values that shape our behavior. Scientists should not hide that fact. Although they want to move away from bias with the idea of a value-free science, in fact they are cloaking values that lead to biases. Such biases emerge, for example, in their studies of IQ and race, free markets and growth, and environmental emissions.

Belief in the importance of adopting a stance of value neutrality is extremely widespread among all scientists. For they wish to emphasize the importance of presenting findings that are not biased by their own preconceptions. Biological scientists financed by pharmaceutical companies doing research on a new drug must follow strict experimental procedures to ensure that they do not exaggerate the drug's effectiveness because they wish to satisfy their sponsors. On the surface, this appears to make good sense, seeming to support the idea of the importance of their avoiding allowing their own values to bias the results of their research.

Yet suppose research financed by pharmaceutical companies that is essential to win the approval of the Food and Drug Administration is incredibly expensive, ruling out potential drugs developed by companies unable to afford that expense. Further, suppose that certain herbal medications are actually very effective, yet since such medicines are outside of the jurisdiction of the FDA and cannot win its approval, their ads will not be seen by the general public as credible.

The result of this current situation is the idea that value neutrality becomes no more than a pretense. For it is the values of large bureaucratic companies that come to be emphasized at the expense of consumers who are hoping for help in fighting their many diseases. It is money, rather than the fight against disease, that wins the day.

Thus, the book quoted above by distinguished philosophers of science is exactly on the mark in its critique of the idea of value neutrality. All of us have values, just as we have emotions, and they cannot be eliminated within the research process. What is crucial is transparency. And that transparency must include informing the public of the kinds of studies on medicines that are ruled out by present-day pharmaceutical research, studies that yield medications that may actually be far more beneficial and far less expensive than those produced by our huge and extremely profitable drug giants.

...

A story about Andy Plotkin's experiences illustrates the combination of an Eastern and Western orientation that anyone can learn to use.

When he attempted to return to full-time academic employment after thirty years in business, countless rejections for full-time instruction and leadership positions left him dejected, doubting his own value as a sociologist, teacher, administrator…"and even as a human being." Following an Eastern orientation, he realized that his defeatism stemmed from unrealistically high aspirations, such as his valuing a full-time academic position.

He learned to take part-time adjunct teaching positions at several colleges that paid little. Working with students, however, was rewarding and increased his self-confidence. This motivated him to learn how to write and produce screenplays, one of which premiered to much acclaim by faculty. He also learned how to write and publish poetry, short stories, and novels, along with published academic journal articles.

As a result, Andy felt good enough to suggest to me the possibility of starting a new school, an idea that later morphed into the idea for writing this book. This involved raising his aspirations one step at a time, giving him the opportunity to find the time to fulfill them as we proceeded with our task. Here, then, was the East-West strategy in action.

...

Neil Weiss has a personal story as well, one that also emphasizes emotions:

> As an example using teachers, the bureaucratic teacher says, "I have my rules." The evolutionary teacher says, "I have my students." For the bureaucratic teacher, very few exceptions are provided because the rules are primary. Only in rare and very exceptional situations will special consideration be given to an individual student.
>
> I consider myself to be an evolutionary teacher because I treat my students as individuals with their own unique characteristics. I apply the rules to them, rather than applying them to the rules. In the process of becoming an evolutionary teacher, I introduced the element of "heart" into the analysis. The bureaucratic personality has "head" and "hand," but is missing "heart."
>
> As I developed into an evolutionary teacher, I introduced "heart" by getting to know who my students are, with their special goals and interests, and special challenges and needs. Over time I have been able to increase my awareness of my students by learning to see more and more aspects of them, including their personalities, so that I can see where their behavior comes from.
>
> When a student has a problem with the course requirements, I am able to put the situation into the perspective of his or her personal issues. For example, I had a student who was constantly late with assignments. It was caused by the new baby in the family and the need for him to support his wife in addition to his work responsibilities.
>
> Knowing that, I was able to support him through the period he needed to deal with the situation. He then was able to catch up and do well thereafter. The bureaucratic teacher does not want to know about those problems, and just follows the established rules about due dates and deadlines.

Neil is emphasizing here his interacting with students, by contrast with remaining isolated from them. Recall, for example, Marx's essay on alienation or isolation, where he focused on the individual's physical, biological, social, and personality isolation. It was interaction that Marx suggested implicitly is important for the worker. You might remember the emphasis on internal interaction, or the interaction among ideas, as described by C. Wright Mills. Also think of the emphasis on external interaction, or the interaction among people, by the Medicis during the period of the Renaissance; think also of the librarian who developed the idea that people could check out a person and not just a book.

Yet generally we fail to understand the power of the Medici Effect as equaling the importance of the integration of the knowledge to be found in books and articles.

...

It is the power of human interaction to help us learn how to solve problems that we must bring to the fore, as illustrated by our favorite storyteller, Tom Savage.

Most of us have experienced at our front doors, at the mall or in the airport, an individual asking the most personal of questions, "Have you been Saved?"

The Reverend Lieutenant always has been able to respond in affirmation, "Yes, Praise Jesus, I have been Saved!"

Proof of this fact goes back to the Calvary Baptist Church, San Bernardino, California, in the mid-1940s. Here, in the eyes of a seven-year-old child, once a month a miracle occurred:

"At the front of a large sanctuary sat the choir. Behind the choir, a curtain, that, when drawn, revealed our beloved pastor, Dr. Van Osdel, in a beautiful white robe, standing in four feet of water which served as the baptismal vehicle for a rite of total immersion. No just sprinkling of water here.

"Now the miracle consisted of the fact that not two minutes after administering these baptisms, Dr. Van Osdel came back into the sanctuary with no evidence of a drop of water on his person. How could this be? I had to investigate, for curiosity is the chief characteristic for both philosopher and cop!

"At the conclusion of the service, with everyone gone, I crept to the back of the church, went up some wet, wooden stairs, and, aha, miracle-mystery solved.

"There, hanging on a hook, was a fly-fisherman's rubber wading suit. That's how the minister managed to stay so dry.

"Unfortunately, our story and detective investigation does not end here. I decided I wanted to try the suit on myself.

"Three sizes too large for me, as I entered the baptismal tank, so the water began to fill the suit.

"Soon, I was thrashing about, because I didn't know how to swim, and the suit was dragging me down.

"Lucky for me, our sexton heard my cries for help, and he 'Saved me.'" "So, yes, I have been Saved, and I think I learned a valuable lesson.

"The sexton probably can be forgiven for using the Lord's name when he saw the rubber suit at the bottom of the pool that he would have to retrieve.

"Naturally, I wanted the whole thing to be hushed up, but the following Sunday's sermon referred to someone in the Sunday School being 'rescued' and hopefully reformed.

"Yep. I sorta was! But remember, when I was so upset because I thought God allowed the horses to drown, yet enabled Moses and the Israelites to stay high and dry along with Pastor Van Osdel? I was still questioning, instead of conforming."

Young Tom Savage not only was continuing to confront bureaucracy by his challenge to authority. He also rejected a narrow understanding of the mystery of his Pastor's dryness.

He also utilized these learned lessons much later in both his ministerial and law enforcement careers.

...

Tom's ability to solve that mystery at the age of seven yielded optimism about the possibility of solving difficult problems, an optimism that we can all share. Recall his story of Charles Collins, the Ethiopian slave in Aida, blowing kisses to his audience for a full five minutes while they were standing up and cheering him on. That was fame that the audience along with the rest of us deeply desire.

Granting that Charles Collins succeeded in having his fifteen minutes of fame, can one individual actually make much of a difference in changing the world? This is a question that many of us answer negatively, resigning ourselves to the idea that you can't fight City Hall. Yet the historical record tells us a different story.

For example, ancient Rome was famous for its Coliseum shows of cruel and brutal spectacles. Hundreds, even thousands, of men and animals were slaughtered each year. In the beginning, the combatants had been criminals whose lives would be spared if they won. Later, political and religious individuals were sacrificed for having views that brought them into disfavor.

One day, a spectator to these atrocities, a Christian monk named Telemachus, could no longer stomach this blood bath. Jumping into the arena, he ordered the fighters to stop. For a moment, the once wild crowd was stunned into silence. But soon the mood became one of anger. Stones rained down upon him, and Telemachus fell to the ground and died. Days later, however, the conversation in Rome was not about the brave gladiators, but the death of a good man, braver than them all. As a result, the Emperor ordered the fights to cease. That was the last gladiator contest in ancient Rome.

Another individual who changed her society was Susan B. Anthony. She played a pivotal role as a women's rights activist, championing women's suffrage. Raised in a Quaker household, she went on to work as a teacher before becoming a leading figure in the abolitionist and women's voting rights movements. She partnered with Elizabeth Cady Stanton, eventually leading the National Women Suffrage Association. The 19th Amendment giving women the right to vote was named in Anthony's honor.

We might turn to Mother Teresa for another example of someone who, before her death, had made the world a different place. She formed Missionaries of Charity in India, providing a network of homes giving food, medical care, and schooling to abandoned and destitute children, including those with special needs. Known in the Catholic Church as Saint Teresa of Calcutta for her devotional work among the poor and dying, she was awarded the Nobel Prize for Peace in 1979.

Yet another example of one individual who was successful in fighting City Hall brings to mind Lech Walesa, who moved from prison to President of Poland. He is now a retired politician and labor activist, having co-founded and headed the first independent trade union within Poland, in defiance of the Soviet Union. For his fight for worker's rights and freedom, he won the Nobel Peace Prize in 1983, and he served as President of Poland from 1990 to 1995. He is famous for the quote, "I'm on my way to eternity, but as long as I have strength, I don't want to allow the destruction of Poland."

In response to the question, "What can I do?" an existentialist philosopher like Albert Camus answers, "What can't you do?" This is a twentieth-century philosophy that centers on one's potential for controlling one's own destiny through the choices that one makes in everyday life, providing that those choices are based on personal experiences and not on the requirements or wishes of others. Its focus is on the freedom of choice that every individual has.

...

Jonathan H. Turner, a renowned sociological theorist, has centered his research on the emotional experiences of the individual. One of his studies centered on understanding the forces operating on individuals who commit acts of terrorism (2007). What can possibly motivate a person to slaughter innocent people? How can we explain why an individual is able to blow himself or herself up? Here is a key part of Turner's general theory, which has to do with the East-West strategy:

> *The (Simplified) Law of Positive Emotional Energy*: When individuals receive positive sanctions and/or **realize their expectations** in an encounter, they will experience positive emotions.

> *The (Simplified) Law of Negative Emotional Energy:* When individuals receive negative sanctions and/or **fail to realize their expectations** in an encounter, they will experience negative emotions.

> *The (Simplified) Law of Repression and Activation of Defense Mechanisms*: When individuals experience negative emotions, they become more likely to protect self through repression that, over time, leads to the intensification and transmutation of the repressed emotion(s). (in Phillips, ed., 2007: 129; boldface added)

Turner's Law of Positive Emotional Energy includes the idea that people experience positive emotions when they "realize their expectations," that is, when they have little or no gap between what they desire and what they actually achieve. In this way, they follow the Buddha's Eastern strategy of doing away with that gap. Their resulting positive emotions are exactly what the Buddha was attempting to achieve.

Staying with that same Law which Turner proposes, another way for people to come to feel good is by interacting with others who "sanction" or reward them in one way or another. This idea is based on the importance of interaction, as indicated by the Medici Effect and illustrated by Neil in his personal story.

By contrast, the Law of Negative Emotional Energy has to do with people's failure, both to fulfill their expectations by both remaining with an aspirations-fulfillment gap, as well as receiving negative sanctions from others. This results in people's negative emotions.

As for Turner's Law of Repression and Activation of Defense Mechanisms, when people experience negative emotions, initially they tend to "repress" those emotions. This follows Freudian theory, with its emphasis on people's repression of problems that they are unable to solve. Over time, however, that repression can intensify those negative emotions and lead to powerful forms of aggression.

On a positive note, there is now hard evidence for the effectiveness of long-term psychoanalysis, based on the work of Freud and his followers, in helping the individual deal with such problems (Leichsenring and Rabung, 2008). People can learn over time to raise up to the surface their patterns of emotional repression and learn to deal with their resulting aggressive behavior.

...

Thomas J. Scheff, another well-known sociological theorist, has focused on learning about our emotions, examining in particular the rise of Adolph Hitler in his Bloody Revenge: Emotions, Nationalism, and War (1994). Hitler has referred in his Mein Kampf to the Treaty of Versailles after having described the Treaty as an instrument of "abject humiliation." Scheff quotes this passage that follows:

> How could every single one of these points have been burned into the brain and emotion of this people, until finally in sixty million heads, in men and women, a common sense of shame and a common hatred would have become a single fiery sear of flame, from whose heat a will as hard as steel would have risen and a cry burst forth: Give us arms again!...If at the beginning of the War and during the War twelve or fifteen thousand of these Hebrew corrupters of the people had been held under poison gas, as happened to hundreds of thousands of our very best German workers in the field, the sacrifice of millions at the front would not have been in vain. On the contrary: twelve thousand scoundrels eliminated in time might have saved the lives of a million real Germans, valuable for the future. (1943: 632, 679)

Scheff refers to the fact that the Treaty of Versailles transferred large portions of German territory to other nations, excluded Germany from the League of Nations as an "unworthy" state, and required Germany to pay large sums of reparations for the war, as well as to confess sole responsibility for having caused World War I. Largely as a result, inflation became rampant throughout the country.

Following Turner's Law of Negative Emotional Energy, it appears that, largely as a result of that treaty, a significant proportion of Germans experienced a wide aspirations fulfillment gap as a result of their economic problems. In addition, the treaty conveyed to them negative sanctions. The result was negative emotions, such as the shame that Hitler cites.

As for Turner's Law of Repression and Activation of Defense Mechanisms, the quote reveals enormous hatred, directed in particular against Jews. Scheff's own analysis advances the idea that intense shame can easily lead to extreme aggression in "shame-rage" cycles at a national level.

...

Yet another of Tom Savage's stories can help us move from pessimism to optimism about the human being's potentials for personal development.

> Midnight. Alone in my patrol car, bored out of my mind. It had been an hour since my last call. Now, suddenly, over my Sheriff Department's radio, I hear: 'Zone Five—BOLO (Be On Lookout). A valuable Great Dane puppy has escaped from its home. Owner frantic—his address, 1214 Gulfgate Drive.'

> As I am writing all of this down, guess who comes trotting into my headlights? Right. The lost puppy! I opened my car door, he hops in, happy to have been found. I call headquarters: 'Dispatch. I have the suspect in custody.' This is followed by a flood of microphone clicking, a form of friendly harassment from my fellow deputies.

> Off I went to return the lost Great Dane to his proper home. Before I departed the owner, I said: 'My favorite breed of dog is a Great Dane. If you and your wife ever want to take off for a little weekend vacation, I'm ready, willing, and able to doggie sit.' But, for now, the case was closed. Yet I knew there would be a can of dog food in my locker at the end of my shift. And, yes, it was there!

> No word from the dog's owners for over a year. Then, the call came. 'Was I serious about taking care of Maximillian, the dog's name, over the weekend?' 'Yep,' I said. And Max and I bonded immediately, played together over a fun-filled day, then finally retired for the night.

> Now, neither Max nor I wore pajamas, so when a wet nose pushed into my ear at two a.m., I knew someone needed, wanted, to go out to do his thing. I got up, put a collar and leash on him, walked across the swimming pool area to the pool door, opened it to let Max out, when a rabbit bolted across the yard. Max jumped after him, pulling me outside. The pool door closed and locked, leaving me standing there stark naked with this dumb dog. I could already see the morning newspaper headlines: 'Sheriff's Lieutenant Exposed.'

> What to do? I knew the next door neighbor had a key, and glancing over to his pool patio, I spotted a dress, draped over a chair. His pool door was unlocked, so I entered and reluctantly put on the dress, went to the front door and rang the bell. A man and woman came to the door.

> 'I'm sorry,' I said. 'I'm taking care of Max, and I have accidently locked myself out of the house. Could I please borrow your key?'

"No problem," said the man, completely ignoring my attire. But his wife, with wide disapproving eyes, kept looking at me. Finally she said: "You know, I have a dress just like yours." I wanted to say, "No shit," but I remembered having had my mouth washed out with soap by my mother when I was a kid, just for having called a grouchy neighbor an old poop!

The man gave me his key. I went back and got dressed, returned the dress and key. The weekend passed with no further incidents. The owners returned. I never said anything. And, thus, my story ends.

One thing, though. I was never asked to doggie-sit again. I believe that neighbor went and blew the whistle on me, asking who the transvestite was that had taken care of Max.

Tom told me another true story that sharply contrasts with his own. A professor who was about to receive an important award for his publications that very evening experienced a fire in the home where he lived with his wife. All of his and his wife's clothing was destroyed except for a single dress.

As a result, he decided to skip the awards ceremony despite his desire to be there. He was not about to brave homophobic prejudices and his own fear and shame of appearing in a woman's dress. Did he even think of the applause that he could have received if he had dared to confront his negative emotions successfully, appeared at the ceremony, and explained what had happened? How many males would have been able to put on that dress?

For Tom, a similar situation had yielded an entirely different outcome. How did he succeed in conquering his own fear and shame that must have accompanied his vision of his neighbor's seeing him in a dress?

I might hazard a guess. Tom was able to weigh the two circumstances—appearing in a dress, and appearing naked—against one another. Perhaps his policing experiences had taught him that the kind of realism illustrated by a minimal aspirations-fulfillment gap was an absolute requirement in his job. Also, his having reached the rank of lieutenant illustrated approval from his colleagues. Thus, following Turner's Law of Positive Emotional Energy, the positive emotions he had developed in himself and received from others gave him the personal confidence that was lacking in the professor who was afraid to attend his awards ceremony.

The result was nothing less than a "profile in courage." It was an illustration of his ability to develop passionate personal commitment to using rationality to solve problems.

...

A story centering on the power of emotions to solve problems is about a drunk who left the bar, deciding to take a shortcut through a nearby graveyard to go home, and ended up falling into a recently-dug open gravesite. In his inebriated state, trying to get out was an exercise in futility.

A second drunk also chose the same shortcut, and he too fell into the grave. As he tried to scramble out, the first drunk tapped him on the shoulder and said, "It's no use. You can't get out of here!" But, in one frightened leap, he was out. Amazing how the right motivation enables us to accomplish unimaginable feats.

Continuing with our accentuating the positive in this chapter on deepening emotional development, we turn to a recent book: Andreas Reckwitz's *The Invention of Creativity: Modern Society and the Culture of the New* (2017). Reckwitz, the recipient of the 2019 Leibniz Prize, claims that the idea of creativity and efforts to practice it have become a basic organizing principle in our modern world.

He argues that it was in the 1980s that there was a convergence around this idea from fields such as art, psychology, and urban planning. Further, he discusses the development of an "aesthetic economy, with the expectation of innovation across all parts of organizations. Workers are motivated by the promise of labor that is genuinely fulfilling and "self-actualizing."

He further discusses the "culturalization of urban life." Overall, there is an emphasis on the power of culture to shape what is going on throughout society. He refers back to the "counterculture" developed by students in the 1960s, and forward to what he calls "countercultural urbanism," illustrated by urban art scenes.

Reckwitz's focus on the power of culture can remind us of the work of Antonio Gramsci (1971), whose *Prison Notebooks* emphasized the "cultural hegemony" of the ruling class—by contrast with Marx's emphasis on the economic system—as the basis for their dominance

Reckwitz succeeds in developing a vision of all this cultural emphasis on creativity as pointing to a direction for people to live up to their full potential. On the other hand, there are winners and losers in the quest for recognition of people's creative achievements. And his outward-oriented focus on audience leaves the question hanging as to what is to be done with those who fail in the effort to secure an audience.

More telling as a criticism is: What is to be done with the rest of us who are sitting in that vast auditorium, watching the creative people on the stage? Can we also become creative? If so, how? Do we need an audience to help us financially and encourage us? If not, how are we to proceed to fulfill our own potential?

And how are we all to deal with the incredible power of bureaucratic structures? The students with their countercultural efforts during the 1960s, with their focus on the power of love and flower power, and their leaders who were supposedly non-leaders, found out that they could not get very far when their idealistic new communities started to collapse.

This is by no means to disparage the new emphasis on creativity that Reckwitz discusses, for those involved are pointing in the same direction as your authors in this book. We applaud any attempt to point toward more emphasis on the incredible potential of every single human being.

...

Our understanding should be widened here. We can cite not only the limitations of Reckwitz's ideas but, in addition, the limitations of all the other ideas advanced in this chapter, starting with those of the Buddha.

We see the achievements of all those discussed in this chapter as stepping stones that reach up toward our basic conclusions. This includes your authors' experiences at earlier times.

One such experience had to do with Tom's favorite aunt, Lillian, God love her. In her late eighties she became a victim of a full-blown case of Alzheimer's disease. It was difficult to keep her entertained because her attention span was so short. Fortunately, this void was filled by a passion to be taken out for a ride in his family car.

On one beautiful spring day, out for a pleasant drive, they passed a mansion up for sale at a cool five point two million dollars, and the real estate agency was holding an Open House. In we drove, up the long driveway, and quickly signed up for an escorted tour of this magnificent residence. It took almost a half hour to completely inspect the home.

At the end, the realtor turned to them and said, "Well, what do you think?" And Lillian replied, "We'll take it!" With eyes now wide open with delight, our poor agent was already mentally picking out the color of the new Mercedes-Benz his commission would allow him to purchase. Unfortunately, Tom had to burst his fantasy balloon by turning to Lillian and saying, "Now, darling, we have a few more houses to see before we make a final decision." She agreed, and they departed from an agent still filled with prayerful hope.

A short time later, after an ice cream stop, Tom said, "I think we have to skip the idea of buying a new house." Lillian replied, "What house?" Tom doesn't know the saint who is responsible for watching over forgetfulness, but to his or her altar he plans to go to light a candle of deep appreciation. Certainly, Lillian is not alone in her lack of clear thinking, if we are to judge from what we read in the newspapers from one day to the next.

...

Tom admits that when he functioned as a sheriff's deputy and later as a lieutenant, he wondered whether it would ever be possible for society to solve the many serious problems that he encountered.

At the present time, however, Tom has managed to move away from his former pessimism about the power resting in all of our hands to solve society's deepest concerns.

The rest of us can join Tom's movement away from pessimism and toward optimism. Once we develop a vision of an alternative to a way of life that is responsible for our pessimism, we are able to move toward optimism. This requires us to learn to transform our capacities to solve problems into abilities. Just as Marx wrote, "The philosophers have only interpreted the world in various ways; the point is to change it."

Part 3: Action ("Hand")

CHAPTER 5

The Problem: Our Bureaucratic Way of Life

PLATO'S ALLEGORY OF THE CAVE

The most famous extended metaphor developed throughout all of Western history is Plato's allegory of prisoners in a cave, who represent us humans:

> Imagine men to be living in an underground cave-like dwelling place, which has a way up to the light along its whole width, but the entrance is a long way up. The men have been there from childhood, with their neck and legs in fetters, so that they remain in the same place and can only see ahead of them, as their bonds prevent them from turning their heads.

> Light is provided by a fire burning some way behind and above them. Between the fire and the prisoners…there is a path across the cave and along this a low wall has been built, like the screen at a puppet show in front of the performers who show their puppets above it…See then also men carrying along the wall, so that they overtop it, all kinds of artifacts, statues of men, reproductions of other animals…

> Do you think, in the first place, that such men could see anything of themselves and each other except the shadows which the fire casts upon the wall of the cave in front of them?…Altogether then, I said, such men would believe the truth to be nothing else than the shadows of the artifacts?…

> The men below had praise and honours from each other, and prizes for the men who saw most clearly the shadows that passed before them, and who could best remember which usually came earlier and which later. (1974: 168-169)

The men cannot see themselves, which is exactly what we have emphasized is the situation of the human race. Readers, you might recall that Socrates, Plato's teacher, believed that the unexamined life is not worth living. Yet here we have the prisoners—like ourselves—unable to examine themselves. All that they can see are shadows on the cave wall in front of them.

Isn't the failure of sociologists to study the individual, to explore the nature not just of the group or society, exactly what I claimed is true in my essay for *Contemporary Sociology?*

Doesn't the *kaizen* ideal of continuing improvement center on what the individual worker is capable of doing and should be doing?

Didn't Marx's analysis of alienation in the workplace show how the individual comes to be divorced from every one of our basic structures: physical, personality, biological and social?

Isn't it true that Gurdjieff's student, P. D. Ouspensky, found that the individual only rarely departs from attention to the outer world?

Aren't the above ideas no more than a few examples of our focus on the individual throughout this book as a whole? For instance, we might think of our treatment of *The Wizard of Oz*, Tom's Sunday school story, our loss of the world of oral culture, the individual as a scientist in everyday life, and C. Wright Mills' vision of the individual's "sociological imagination."

Returning to Plato's allegory, we might look to the fact that the prisoners are blind not only to themselves, but also to the actual objects around them, for they see no more than shadows on the cave wall in front of them. Here, once again, our book emphasizes the very idea Plato stresses.

Aren't we largely blind to the existence of our double crisis of meaninglessness and escalating world problems, especially given that we have developed no alternatives?

Isn't it the case that we are blind to the powerful concepts of the social sciences that could help us to understand our situation and then do something about it?

Doesn't our blindness extend to a lack of awareness of the many times that we have only narrowly escaped World War III and the possibility of nuclear annihilation?

Following the Buddha, aren't we blind to just how wide the gap is between our many aspirations and our ability to fulfill them?

Aren't we also blind to the fact that we share with Nazi Germany and the Stalinist USSR a bureaucratic way of life?

Coming back once again to Plato's cave, is it true that we have no freedom, for we are prisoners who are tied up and cannot even move our heads?

At this time in history, do we feel free to move away from our pessimism about the future and toward optimism?

Are we free to realize that unanticipated consequences dominate our lives?

Does our freedom extend to learning how to make full use of language and the scientific method in our everyday lives?

Following McQuarie, Gramsci and Reckwitz, are we free to realize the enormous power of culture?

Can we dare to be sufficiently free to do what Tom did within his Great Dane story, and risk being seen as a sexual pervert?

...

An illustration of the nature of our degree of freedom is provided by Jack Benny. A comic sketch has him entering a department store at Christmas time, shopping for a gift for his wife. At the jewelry counter he selects a watch. It is the cheaper one for

$12.95, not the one for $300.00. "An excellent choice, sir," says the clerk. "This particular watch comes with an indestructible crystal. Here, see for yourself," handing Jack a small hammer.

"Oh, I don't know," says Jack. "Go ahead, suggests the clerk. Give it a whack," which Jack does, smashing the watch into tiny pieces.

"Do you want that gift wrapped?" asks the clerk. "Gift wrapped?" stammers Jack. "I don't even want it now. I want my money back!"

"I'm sorry, sir. Company policy. You broke it, you bought it," says the clerk. "Well, that's a fine policy," says Jack.

"You walked in here, Twinkle-Toes, no one forced you," retorts the clerk.

"This is ridiculous. I want to see the manager," demands Jack. The clerk calls over the floor manager. "Mr. Walker. This man just broke this watch, and now refuses to pay for it."

"Well, she told me to do it," exclaims Jack.

"And, do we do whatever people tell us to do?" inquires the floor manager.

"I will stay right here and shout out to every customer around here that this store has treated me dishonestly until I get my money back. I'll also write to the newspapers and call the local television station about what thieves you people are," shouts Jack. "Worse, I'm going to sic Fred Allen on you," he adds.

Without another word being said, the manager motions to the clerk to return Jack's money, which she does, and Jack moves off in a huff.

Jack actually was free to behave in a way that enabled him to get his money back. That required him to become so highly motivated that he threatened to act in a way which few of us would dare to copy. He illustrated the power of personality structure.

But what about the power of social structure or, more specifically, bureaucracy? Both the clerk and the store manager colluded to deprive him of what was rightfully his, even though they were well aware that it was the clerk and not Jack who was responsible for the smashed watch. Apparently, the Company policy of the store was to do whatever it could to increase its profits, and the public be damned.

Of course, not all stores would act like this one did. But aren't they all organized in a bureaucratic way, where they all focus on maximizing profits? Isn't a focus on their bottom line, rather than the welfare of clients, the name of the game for them? Wouldn't most customers fail to confront the clerk and the store manager, as Jack did?

Jack's behavior was exactly what the viewer of Jack's routine applauded. He or she might even fantasize behaving just as Jack did in that situation. But that fantasy is far from the reality of what would actually happen if the viewer were to appear in those circumstances.

Readers might recall Verdi's opera, "Aida," and the unanticipated performance of Charles Collins, "The Great," achieving his fifteen minutes of fame. That local audience cheered him on for a full five minutes, much like the reaction of those who viewed Jack Benny's sketch.

Who among that opera audience would have dared to behave as Charles did? They gloried in Charles' ability to defy the opera company, for they too had had enough of their daily subservience to the powers that be. But the exuberance of that very defiance suggests just how much the audience members had experienced disappointment, unhappiness, fear, and even despair in their daily dealings with huge organizations.

...

A book that updates Vidich and Bensman's analysis of the fantasy world of the Springdalers is Antony Alumkal's *Paranoid Science: The Christian Right's War on Reality* (2017). This one-sided analysis does not reflect our own view of the importance of religion in modern society.

Alumkal argues that the political focus of the Christian Right is to give battle to any scientific findings that fail to conform to their own interpretation of biblical statements. He grants that not all conservative Christians or supporters of their political efforts agree with such beliefs, yet he sees that the influence of this group on American politics is enormous.

Alumkal further sees the agenda of the Christian Right as extremely wide-ranging, including claims about the Earth's origins, the rejection of global warming, disbelief of same-sex attraction, conspiracy theories about those opposing their views, a war on textbooks disagreeing with their views, undermining the theory of evolution and substituting a belief in intelligent design, and seeing themselves as key defenders of American morality and exceptionalism. Following Alumkal, all of these views are greatly accentuated by this group's outsized access to social media of all kinds.

Actually, your authors believe that there is no need for the belief that science and religion are necessarily opposed. Albert Einstein claimed: "Science without religion is lame, religion without science is blind." A union between science and religion was well illustrated by the original Buddha.

Further, religion can teach us the huge power of ritual behavior, just as social scientists have taught us of the importance of social structures, and just as we have emphasized the power of personality structure.

Religion can also teach us the importance of attention to the beliefs and feelings of the individual human being, and thus help us move away from a focus on the impersonal organization, the group, and society as a whole. This is illustrated by the biblical idea that man was made in the image of God.

If we pay attention to the religions of all peoples, past and present, then we are moving in a truly interdisciplinary direction and have much to learn.

Religious people of ancient times, such as those who built the pyramids and Stonehenge, illustrate for us the tremendous potential for achievement of all of us.

The moral guidance that religion offers us, as illustrated by the Ten Commandments and the Buddha's Four Noble Truths, can help us develop a direction in life far more than all the achievements of the physical sciences, along with relativistic and postmodern theories.

Religion can help us develop a sense of community that the biophysical sciences fail to yield.

At the same time, following Einstein, science has much to teach religion. Religion without science is blind to how society, making use of the social sciences, might actually help people fulfill their potential.

It is social science that can become a powerful tool to help religious followers find deeper meaning in their lives.

It is the scientific theory of evolution that can help those of all religious persuasions to move toward their own personal evolution.

It is the breadth of an interdisciplinary scientific method, including the ideas of lay people, no less than what has been published, that can make full use of the full range of experiences of people following our many different religions.

It is the incredible power of that method which can help us to solve the deepening problems of society and the individual. For it can help us to move away from our ignorance, and our immersion in fantasies where it is evil individuals who are responsible for whatever is wrong with the world.

...

We have by no means completed our analysis of bureaucracy as the basic problem of contemporary life. There are indeed many unsolved and even increasing problems in contemporary society which we see as closely linked to that pattern of bureaucratic behavior. We shall now focus on two of the problems we see as of special importance: our patterns of addiction and aggression.

ADDICTION

We define addiction as *habits that subordinate individual development to dependence on an outward orientation that yields a limited way of life.* The close link between addiction and our way of life makes it extremely difficult to eliminate addictive behavior without changing that way of life. This helps to explain why narrow efforts to eliminate addiction generally fail.

Addiction yields a limited way of life. Have you noticed that in our modern times, the art of conversation has been lost? Go to any food court at your local shopping mall. People seated across from one another at tables are not talking. They are texting!

And then there is watching television, e-mailing from many digital gadgets, surfing the computer, writing books, talking on the telephone, exercising, running, walking, seeing physicians, and shopping, Of course, all of these activities can be most useful in moderation, but when carried to excess they prevent one from fulfilling the full range of one's possibilities as a human being.

...

Let us now move from these general ideas about the forces behind addiction to a genuine crisis in modern society: the rapidly increasing number of overdose deaths linked to opioid addiction. The attraction of opioids is that they produce pleasurable sensations and relieve pain. Opioids include the illicit drug heroin along with such prescription pain relievers as oxycodone, hydrocodone, codeine, morphine and fentanyl. Carfentanyl is a particularly deadly additive to the heroin sold on the streets, for minute amounts can be deadly for humans.

For many, using opioids at first was for pain. Then others found emotional relief for stress, but ended up just using them as an escapist recreational drug trip. Soon, however, fun became an addiction.

Drug overdose is the leading cause of accidental death in the US, with 52,404 deaths resulting from overdoses in 2015. Opioid overdoses resulted in most of those deaths, with 20,101 related to prescription pain relievers and 12,990 related to heroin. Between 1999 and 2015 the opioid death rate increased by over 300%. All of this is happening despite our "war on drugs."

This drug problem extends to the problem of recovery from addiction. We know almost nothing about the effectiveness of treatment programs. Indeed, the question might even be raised as to whether any effective recovery program presently exists. The lack of statistics on recovery from addiction is an appalling situation.

...

For an illustration of what addiction's outward orientation can lead to, we turn to an event that is most difficult to understand. It is the story about Anthony Bourdain, the extremely successful chef who introduced and starred in the 2013 popular TV series, *Parts Unknown*. He committed suicide in 2017.

Earlier, Bourdain had an addiction problem that he had been successful in overcoming. In 2016 he told People magazine, "I wake up in the morning looking at beautiful vistas and doing interesting things, but the truth of the matter is I'm alone for most of that time" (Calderone, 2018: 24).

During an episode of *Parts Unknown*, he asked in a voice-over: "What do you do after your dreams come true?" (27).

On his nightstand he kept a copy of Graham Greene's autobiography, which includes these words: "Sometimes I wonder how all those who do not write, compose or paint can manage to escape the madness, the melancholia, the panic fear which is inherent in the human condition" (27).

Despite Bourdain's having abandoned substance abuse, these quotes indicate his continuing outward orientation, which is so central to patterns of addiction. There is his concern with loneliness. If we assume that his dreams coming true indicated his financial success, coupled with his achievement of fame, then an outward orientation is illustrated once again.

Let us recall that it is the very nature of addiction to "subordinate individual development to dependence on an outward orientation that yields a limited way of life." Perhaps the achievement of wealth and fame, which points one outward, illustrates a limited way of life. For it succeeds in neglecting key aspects of one's own personal development. And perhaps Bourdain's assumption that extremely negative emotions are "inherent in the human condition" was central to his committing suicide.

Here is a story about addiction that Tom created to help those whose lives had been destroyed:

> Suppose you had grown up in Gopher-Prairie (with gratitude and apology to Sinclair Lewis for having borrowed the name).
>
> O.K. You have been born in Gopher-Prairie, Minnesota. The name says it all. Nothing ever happens in Gopher-Prairie. If one word captures the spirit of this town, that word would be 'boredom.'
>
> But, a whispered rumor has it, especially among the young, that a carnival is on its way, with a ride (a drug) that should provide quite a thrill. Suddenly, little old Gopher-Prairie has become electrified in anticipation, long before the event itself has occurred.
>
> The carnival arrives with its roller-coaster ride (a drug), and, yes, the rush from that first drop takes your breath away. It's all true. What a thrill. But after the initial plunge, the other hills aren't all that exciting. No problem. Just run around, get on the ride, and do it again and again. The real problem, however, is this. After fifty rides, the thrill is gone. This, too, has become, 'ho hum, been there, done that.'
>
> But, again the whispered rumor has reached your ears, telling you the carnival owners are bringing an even higher roller-coaster (stronger drug) with an even greater rush. So, what's the problem?
>
> The problem is that our bodies are smarter than we are. When experiences cause too much stress in the system, the body defends itself by building up a tolerance for invading experiences, including drugs. So, no matter how high we ultimately get, inevitably, our wild ride will bring us down to where we began this escapist behavior. We end up right back in Gopher-Prairie, Minnesota.
>
> What, then, can we do if the only world we have known is Gopher-Prairie? How can we shape a destiny that does not take us back down to boredom?

Another example of addiction has to do with modernity which Tom remembers from his ministerial experiences.

> A modern church, up to date with all manner of electronic gadgets, including multiple TV screens, a stereo sound system, a pulpit that would swing to the side, and a lectern that could sink to the floor to allow a wide open space for singers, dancers, and drama productions.

One Sunday as the morning lesson from scripture was being read, a mechanical glitch occurred, causing the lectern to sink slowly back into the floor, with the desperate reader slowly sinking down with it. My mind immediately flashed to the scene from The Wizard of Oz where the Wicked Witch of the West, having been hit by water tossed on her by Dorothy, started crying, "I'm melting, I'm melting!"

Almost all of us are addicted to the gadgets of modernity, just as the church reader could not imagine doing without his lectern, and thus started to sink down with it. We think that we cannot possibly live without a new car, a dishwasher and disposal, a smartphone, a very large flat-screen TV, clothing illustrating the very latest fashion, an updated computer, and much more. We encourage more and more housing "development" that crowds out our open spaces and forces many of us to live in shadow. We see Amish people riding their bicycles, and we look down on them.

OK, what is the price of this focus on so-called modernity? Is this really further human development? Or does it illustrate a one-sided outward orientation that hides from us our failure to truly move toward personal and world evolution with a more balanced approach to life that does not neglect inner development? Can we continue to be smug about our achievement of what has become an addiction to so-called modernity?

We move now from the problem of addiction to that of aggression.

AGGRESSION

Tom provides us with another of his experiences as a deputy sheriff. This one illustrates a type of aggression.

Midnight. A local merchant had suffered several burglaries during the past year, so he had chain-linked his property and had a security business provide a guard dog. A careless employee had failed to properly secure the main gate at closing, and now the guard dog was loose, chasing both cars and individuals as he had been trained to do. Tom was dispatched with his partner to secure the scene. They quickly located the dog and had the dispatcher call the security agency to come and get the dog. There was no immediate threat, and in fifteen minutes a van arrived, and an elderly African-American gentleman got out to collect the animal.

At this point, Tom's partner stuck his elbow into Tom's side and said, "Watch this. German Shepherds hate colored people." What an interesting concept, thought Tom. With all of his education and years of training, he had never heard such an idea before. Well, this "colored people" just happened to be the dog's trainer, and with an obvious sense of relief and happiness the dog raced over to his master, put his paws up on the man's chest, kissed him with one lick to the cheek, and obediently hopped into the van. To which Tom's partner exclaimed, "What a stupid dog!"

We can guess that Tom's partner not only was deeply prejudiced against black people, but that such prejudice also involved negative emotions like hatred. We can also guess that he remained unable to move out of his fantasy world that stereotyped black people as bad, and himself as good. It is all too easy for those of us who believe deeply in equality to succumb to hating Tom's partner. Instead, however, we can come to see him—and ourselves as well, despite our beliefs that we are completely free of prejudice—as victims of a way of life that emphasizes persisting hierarchy.

...

Charles Dickens' *A Christmas Carol* (1843/1991) can help us to understand more fully the problem of aggression. We may all recall Ebenezer Scrooge, that lonely miser concerned only with money. His aggression is well illustrated by his treatment of his clerk, Bob Cratchit. However, he was completely transformed by visits from the Ghosts of Christmas Past, Christmas Present, and Christmas Yet to Come. For those visits helped him to understand his past and present as well as his possible future.

Scrooge learns from the Ghost of Christmas Past that he was a solitary child, neglected by friends. The girl he had loved leaves him with these words: "I have seen your nobler aspirations fall off one by one, until the master-passion, Gain, engrosses you...Our contract is an old one. It was made when we were both poor and content to be so, until, in good season, we could improve our worldly fortune by our patient industry.

"You *are* changed. When it was made, you were another man...I release you. With a full heart, for the love of him you once were."

The Ghost of Christmas Present takes him to the Christmas meal at his clerk's house, where Bob Cratchit and his wife toast Ebenezer Scrooge. But there is no heartiness to their proceedings. A dark shadow had been cast over their party at the mention of his name.

As for the Ghost of Christmas Yet to Come, Scrooge is taken to a churchyard and reads upon the stone of a neglected grave his own name, Ebenezer Scrooge. His death is followed by the theft of his belongings, including the very blankets required to bury him. He also learns of the death of Tiny Tim, which would have been averted had Scrooge offered to help the family.

In the musical version of this story, which is just called *Scrooge*, he finds himself outside his wretched house, with the whole neighborhood singing a song,

"Thank you very much," which Scrooge joins in with hand-clapping joy. What Scrooge fails to realize is they are rejoicing in his death, and he doesn't even see his coffin being removed from his house. All the people who owe him money are certainly "thanking him very much" for having passed on.

Although we all can remember the upbeat ending of the story, when Scrooge has a complete change of heart as a result of these experiences, we cannot expect that the Scrooges among us will actually experience visits from such ghosts. We are, then, left with the question of how to understand both the causes of aggression and how to do something about it.

...

Tom's next story, about an experience as a child in San Bernardino, California, centers on an instance of his own aggressive behavior:

> How many of you remember, during your youthful days, having a secret place for club members only, who know the special handshake, the password for entrance, and the secret knowledge known only to club members?
>
> As kids, we had the Skeleton Club. We were fortunate in that the field behind our house had never been built on. This allowed us to dig a five-feet-deep, six-feet-wide, and ten-feet-long hidden fort for all our meetings. We had found discarded broken lumber plus giant cardboard sheets from a nearby construction site, and we used these materials to completely cover our hideout, leaving only a small hole for entrance. All of this had been covered with dirt and, over time, even grass had grown on top.
>
> Now, one of the reasons why California is often called the "Golden State" is that the hot and dry summers turn most fields into a yellow-brown. The problem is that unattended fields pose a high fire risk, where even a carelessly tossed cigarette can cause great damage. To prevent this danger, the county comes out and plows the fields, thus reducing the threat.
>
> One day, I was standing at the corner of the field that hid our fort. A truck and trailer with a plow pulled up, and the county worker began to plow the field, going up and down, back and forth. I remember thinking, "I sure hope he doesn't find our secret fort," but he did. Yet I took some comfort in that he was, I guess, a religious man. Because as he and his tractor disappeared into our fort, I heard him cry out "Jesus Christ!" I still felt that despite his having discovered our secret fort, that this did not mean that he was automatically eligible for club membership.

There is aggression here, for the county worker could have been badly hurt, and Tom could have avoided that possibility by alerting him to the presence of the fort. Why the aggression?

For one thing, Tom's interest in the fort not being discovered was his outward orientation. For another thing, creating the secret fort was a response to the frustration of a childhood where parents called all the shots, deciding how one must live one's life with no consultation with children about what they wanted to do. Thus, outward orientation plus frustration appears to equal aggression.

...

Another of Tom's stories has to do with one of his experiences as a minister. Age brings change, and in later life one's intellectual abilities can begin to suffer. A church member came to him for counseling. At age 90 the Department of Motor Vehicles had sent her a letter requesting that she take a driving test to prove her ability to drive safely. She asked Tom, "Do you think I should tell them I occasionally fall asleep behind the wheel?" "Yes," he said, "be sure to tell them that." She did, ending her driving days and bringing an end to this story.

Tom's parishioner was obviously most anxious to retain her driver's license, as are almost all older drivers, given the importance of that license for maintaining their present independent way of life. Imagine, for example, the loss of your own driver's license. It was that frustration coupled with her outward orientation of requiring the car for external errands that was much of the basis for her aggressive behavior of possibly concealing her falling asleep at the wheel.

...

Readers should know by now that there are no partial solutions to the basic problems of society, whether those be aggression, addiction or any other problem. Yet readers should also know by now that there are general solutions, based on the incredible potentials of every single human being.

There are actual experiments, and not just interview surveys, that have been conducted on us humans that yield deep understanding of the causes of aggression. Due to present day requirements that protect subjects of such studies, many of those conducted in the past cannot be repeated. Even so, we can look to the evidence they have yielded. We stay with the focus of this chapter on the role of our way of life in producing such behavior.

We begin with Stanley Milgram's *Obedience to Authority* (1974). Our focus here is not simply on prejudice or hatred, which is a precursor to physical aggression, but rather is on physical aggression itself.

Milgram, a social psychologist at Yale University, selected 500 individuals from different walks of life in the New Haven area, paying them $4 an hour for their participation in what they thought was a study of learning. Actually, however, it was a study of conformity to authority, exploring the forces that led people—like those in Hitler's bureaucracies—to follow the orders of those in command.

Thus, Milgram was testing the conclusions of Hannah Arendt about the enormous forces for conformity within a bureaucratic way of life. Readers will recall that Arendt believed that we must never forget the central role of the structure of bureaucracy in the slaughter of innocents.

Each of the 500 subjects of the experiments, separated from the others, was required to take on the role of "teacher" to a 47-year-old mild-mannered accountant—a confederate of Milgram—who played the role of "learner." They were given orders by an "experimenter," dressed in a gray technician's coat, with the "experiments" taking place within the vicinity of Yale University.

The experimenter would tell the learner a pair of words, like "blue box," and later the learner would be required to repeat the second word after being told the first word. If the learner failed to respond or gave an incorrect answer, then the teacher was required to use a shock generator to give the learner a 15-volt shock. *And for each additional incorrect answer or silence, the teacher had to shock the learner with 15 additional volts, moving all the way up to the shock generator's maximum of 450 volts.* Unknown to the "teachers," however, the so-called shock generator was a phony instrument that delivered no shocks whatsoever.

When the experiments were completed, Milgram asked an audience of college students, psychiatrists, and other adults their expectations as to the reactions of the subjects of the experiment. Not a single one of the 110 individuals who responded expected any subject to administer a shock greater than 300 volts, and most replied that no one would have gone past 150 volts.

Yet, in fact, fully 65 percent of the experimental subjects continued up to a maximum of 450 volts. One might imagine how they felt about themselves after the experiment was over, especially if they had started with any mental problems. Indeed, it is for this very reason that any such experiment (including the Zimbardo and Levin experiments described in the following pages) can never be repeated, for new standards protecting experimental subjects are now in place.

This experiment illustrates the incredible power of officials thought to be linked to a high-status organization to achieve conformity even in the face of requiring someone to deliver a 450-volt shock on a human being, a huge violation of basic humanistic values.

We all generally think that our own individuality and values would never allow us to simply follow the leader. Yet would we behave the way 65 percent of the subjects of the Milgram experiments behaved? Would we proceed to shock the learner up to the level of 450 volts? The evidence suggests that most of us would follow the value of conformity if an experimenter from a prestigious university ordered us to do so.

A tragedy surrounding the Milgram experiment is not that the "teachers" generally obeyed the experimenter and continued to shock the "learner" with what they believed to be increasingly high voltages up to the point of lethal shocks. It is the fact that people generally would engage in the same kind of conformity under similar circumstances. We have learned to follow our leaders and experts, like lemmings walking behind one another over a cliff to their deaths.

Our real tragedy takes us far beyond the Milgram experiment to our present-day situation. That study is widely known, yet its implications are widely ignored, and that is most shocking. For it points to the idea that the aggressive behavior of those "teachers" is built into the very nature of our society. Aggression appears to be part and parcel of our bureaucratic way of life. Just as Hitler's minions followed their leader in the slaughter of six million Jews and millions of others, apparently we enlightened folk are prone to similar behavior.

We should take into account, however, the necessity of developing an alternative way of life if we are to seriously question our present pattern of behavior. Readers might recall that our most eminent student of bureaucracy, Max Weber, remained unable to emerge with an alternative to bureaucracy, and contemporary social scientists have done no better.

Yet it is our very way of life that has encouraged such failures. For it is an emphasis on narrow specialization with very little integration of knowledge that has stood in the way of our learning how to develop an alternative to bureaucracy.

More specifically, social scientists—paralleling the Springdalers—have been unable to face the impotence of their own overspecialized procedures that they view as completely scientific. Just as the Springdalers proceeded to ignore their own personal behavior by externalizing the self, so also modern social scientists avoid the limitations of their own scientific procedures. They fail to follow Gouldner's vision of reflexivity.

Instead, they could move toward following the actual requirement of the scientific method that knowledge must be integrated. As a result, they could lay the groundwork for the development of understanding throughout society of how to move beyond bureaucracy. Given all the specialized knowledge that presently exists, the basis is already there for such an achievement.

Our fundamental tragedy, then, is the failure of contemporary societies to learn the lessons that the experiment teaches, and then figure out what to do about it. If aggression is built into society, then present efforts to eliminate aggressive behavior, based on the partial or specialized approaches presently in use, simply will not work. What is required is nothing less than a vision of an alternative way of life, and then movement toward that vision.

...

A second experiment, the Stanford Prison Experiment, was dramatized in a 2015 American film with the same title. It was conducted in 1971 at Stanford University under the supervision of psychology professor, Philip Zimbardo.

The focus of this experiment was on the psychological effects of becoming a prisoner or a prison guard. Twenty-four male students were randomly selected to play the role of either prisoner or guard in a mock prison situated in the basement of the Stanford Psychology Department building. The experiment was abruptly stopped after six days, mainly as a result of the extensive abuse of the prisoners by the guards. Here is a brief description of the experiment, as discussed in an article by C. Haney, W. C. Banks, and P. G. Zimbardo (1973):

> The researchers provided the guards with wooden batons to establish their status, clothing similar to that of an actual prison guard (khaki shirt and pants from a local military surplus store), and mirrored sunglasses to prevent eye contact. Prisoners wore uncomfortable ill-fitting smocks and stocking caps, as well as a chain around one ankle. Guards were instructed to call prisoners by their assigned numbers, sewn on their uniforms, instead of by name.

Zimbardo designed the experiment in order to induce disorientation and depersonalization among the prisoners. They were "arrested" at their homes and "charged" with armed robbery. The local Palo Alto police department assisted Zimbardo with the arrests and conducted full booking procedures on the prisoners, which included fingerprinting and taking mug shots.

They were transported to the mock prison from the police station, where they were strip searched and given their new identities. The prisoners were to stay in their cells all day and night until the end of the study. The guards did not have to stay on site after their shift.

The guards and prisoners adapted to their roles far more than Zimbardo expected, stepping beyond predicted boundaries, leading to dangerous and psychologically damaging situations. One-third of the guards were judged to have exhibited "genuine sadistic tendencies," while many prisoners were emotionally traumatized, as five of them had to be removed early from the experiment. (Haney et al.: 4-17)

The Stanford Prison Experiment was supposed to focus on "the psychological effects of becoming a prisoner or a prison guard." In fact, however, it was set up to focus on the psychological effects of becoming a humiliated prisoner or a sadistic guard. As a result, Zimbardo achieved not the goal of understanding the psychological effects of becoming a prisoner or a prison guard, but rather the impact of an extremely bureaucratic way of life on us human beings.

That experiment demonstrated the power of our bureaucratic way of life to yield both sadism and psychological damage. One might quibble with the procedures used in this experiment in an effort to avoid the conclusion that your authors draw: that patterns of aggression are not the property of some quack minority of skinheads or white supremacists whom we can easily dismiss as extremists who reject our way of life. Rather, we see those patterns as nothing less than illustrating the basic structure of our society.

...

Jack Levin was my doctoral student at Boston University. His dissertation had a complicated title, "The Influence of Social Frame of Reference ("head") for Goal Fulfillment ("heart") on Social Aggression" ("hand").

Levin's focus was on learning about the causes of prejudice, which we may understand to be a type of aggression even though it is mental rather than physical. His subjects were 180 freshmen and sophomores in two sections of introductory sociology at Boston University. Early in the semester he measured the students' degree of prejudice against Puerto Ricans.

One of Levin's two basic hypotheses was that outward-oriented students would increase their prejudice against Puerto Ricans if they were frustrated. He measured this bureaucratic orientation by determining whether students compared their grades with the grades of other students rather than with their own previous grades.

He believed that the behavior of the outward-oriented students would be much like being on a see-saw with a Puerto Rican at the opposite end of the see-saw. Being frustrated would be much like being pushed down by the Puerto Rican, while increasing one's prejudice would be much like pushing up while pushing down the Puerto Rican.

Levin's second hypothesis was that students who are somewhat oriented inward or toward their own development—illustrated by comparing their grades to their own previous grades rather than those of other students—would not increase their prejudice against Puerto Ricans if they were frustrated. For they would see themselves on an evolutionary stairway rather than on a see-saw. Aggression against Puerto Ricans would not help them climb that stairway.

Jack created an extremely frustrating experience for all of the students by giving them what they believed to be an aptitude test for success in graduate school. Actually, the "aptitude test" had nothing to do with aptitude for success in graduate school, yet the students believed that it was genuine, based on their answers to questions after the experiment was over. They were given 12 minutes to complete a vocabulary test consisting of 150 difficult items, with many of the words made up by Levin. Every student totally failed the test.

Shortly after this experience, Levin once again measured the students' degree of prejudice against Puerto Ricans. He found that his first hypothesis was indeed correct. The outward-oriented students generally increased their prejudice against Puerto Ricans. Their aggressive behavior was their tool for raising themselves up on their see-saw by putting down the Puerto Ricans on the other end of the see-saw.

His second hypothesis was also confirmed, for the students oriented inward to some extent generally did not increase their prejudice. Levin followed up his experiment with a questionnaire that confirmed his experimental results. He found that the inward-oriented students revealed less hatred against various groups and were less committed to the values of external conformity and narrow specialization than the students who were more outward-oriented.

The significance of this experiment is that Levin created experimentally a microcosm of the macrocosm of contemporary society. Just as Levin organized severe frustration within his experiment, so we are all severely frustrated by an increasing gap between our aspirations or values and their degree of fulfillment within our present way of life.

I see the Levin experiment as evidence that aggression of all kinds is built into the very nature of our way of life, and this includes bullying, terrorism, war, and violent crime, and also prejudice and discrimination, racism, sexism, ethnocentrism and ageism.

There are aspects of our way of life that work against reducing aggression. For example, social science research with very limited breadth will fail to detect such factors as the failure to look inward. And patterns of conformity will prevent researchers from questioning their basic approach to the scientific method.

As I look back on the Levin experiment so many years ago, I must admit that aggression was not limited to the students who increased their prejudice against Puerto Ricans upon being frustrated by their failure on the so-called aptitude test for graduate school. For I recall just how happy Levin felt—along with me, as the chair of his doctoral committee—when he constructed words for the vocabulary test that appeared to be quite genuine yet simply did not exist. We felt free to smile at those invented words, with little empathy for what the students were experiencing upon learning that they had failed the aptitude test.

Our own aggression could be largely explained by this experiment. Just as the students who saw themselves on a seesaw were the ones who increased their prejudice, so Levin and I joined them in our own lack of attention to our own feelings of glee at giving the students words that did not exist. Just as the students were frustrated by their failing the vocabulary test, so were we frustrated by living in a society where our own large and increasing aspirations-fulfillment gap is par for the course.

While we measured the students' aggressive behavior illustrated by their increased prejudice, we failed to be aware of our own aggressive behavior, let alone measure it. We investigators were by no means immune to the immense power over us of our bureaucratically organized way of life.

It is the Levin experiment that points us in this direction. Some of those students at Boston University compared their present grades with their previous grades, revealing a partial inward orientation along with their outward orientation. That in turn inoculated them from increasing their prejudice against Puerto Ricans. They had learned to move off society's see-saw and onto an evolutionary stairway.

An example of aggression illustrated by prejudice, just as in the case of the Levin experiment, was told to Tom as a true story. It took place in a Franciscan monastery, just outside of Florence, Italy. It was told to him by a fellow camper at a Baptist summer camp, because one of the campers was being picked on since he was so small.

A youth of eighteen had entered a Franciscan order which celebrated the values of compassion, charity, love, and service. To his surprise, his fellow monks displayed none of those ideals with him. In fact, he was daily ridiculed, played tricks on, and abused both emotionally and physically. He was tossed around like a plaything, a toy, to the amusement of his brother monks.

Perhaps the monks' excesses could be found in the fact that their newest member was only four feet five inches in height. In today's world, he probably would have been classified as a midget.

One night, an alarm went out. The monastery was on fire. The monks rushed to the door of their dormitory, but it was barred from the outside. The Abbott had done this to prevent any of the monks from being naughty, sneaking off at night to participate in activities totally prohibited.

Believing they were all about to die, the monks fell to their knees in prayer. Suddenly, one monk spied a small window at the back of the hall. Standing on each other's shoulders, they lifted the little monk, with a rope in hand, up to the opening.

Out he scrambled through the window, down the rope, running to open the blocked door.

Out stampeded his fellow brother monks. All had been saved. Now, falling to their knees, as the rest of the monastery was consumed by the flames, the monks again began to pray, not to God or the Virgin, but in confession, asking for forgiveness for their past sins of abuse.

All had learned a valuable lesson that night. You need not be big in order to do great deeds. That lesson sharply contradicted the message that we all learn; namely, it is only those in superior positions, by contrast with the rest of us, who are able to do important things.

Yes, we can learn to move beyond aggression.

We are convinced that, by remaining on our see-saw, we human beings have no future.

We are equally convinced that we all have the capacity to move onto an infinite stairway. And we believe we have a direction for helping us step onto that stairway.

In our final chapter, we carry further our vision of breaking the bonds that keep us in our cave of ignorance. Once again, we will use the tools of the scientific method and the power of language. But our major tool for moving toward that vision will be the infinite capacities of the individual human being.

CHAPTER 6

The Solution: An Evolutionary Way of Life

The absolutely incredible achievement of Mahatma Gandhi was Britain's granting independence to India in August, 1947. Of course, Gandhi did not achieve this all by himself, yet he was by far the single individual most responsible for this blow to British colonialism that paved the way for other anti-colonial movements throughout the world.

Such movement away from persisting hierarchy toward equality was a huge advance for the peoples on the Indian subcontinent, away from a way of life shared by colonial peoples throughout the world. Gandhi's achievement, portrayed by Joan V. Bondurant in *Conquest of Violence,* also had repercussions for the later nonviolent efforts of Martin Luther King, Jr.

The young Gandhi was not wealthy, for he was born into a poor merchant caste family. He was also dark-skinned, by contrast with the dominant white caste. And he was thrown into the latter part of the 19th century in a British colony at a time when colonialism was dominant throughout the world..

Gandhi's "Satyagraha" movement was the basis for his overall approach to freeing India from British rule: This was a political movement and not just a philosophy. "Satya" means truth, and "Satyagraha" means insistence on or reliance on truth. It arms the individual with moral power rather than physical power.

Gandhi stated that the most important battle he had to fight was overcoming his own demons, fears, and insecurities. It is here that we have evidence of his using the full power of Eastern thought with its focus on individual development.

As for where Gandhi gained his motivation for his political battles, we can look to his many experiences of being the object of discrimination by the British, as well as by their betrayal of his trust in them.

For example, after he had obtained a law degree in London and moved to South Africa, he was not allowed to sit with European passengers in the stagecoach and told to sit on the floor near the driver. When he refused, he was beaten. Elsewhere, he was kicked into a gutter for daring to walk near a house.

Once he was thrown off a train after refusing to leave the first-class. Another time the magistrate of a Durban court ordered Gandhi to remove his turban, which he refused to do. Also, Indians in South Africa were not allowed to walk on public footpaths. Once without warning he was kicked by a police officer out of the footpath and onto the street.

But that was by no means all of the examples of discrimination that Gandhi experienced. White officials denied him his rights. The press and those in the streets bullied him, calling him names like "parasite," "semi-barbarous," "canker," "squalid coolie," and "yellow man." Sometimes people would actually spit on him.

There was also the British betrayal of their promise to grant India self-government after World War I as a reward for India's helping the British during that war. That help was not minor. Even during the earlier Boer War, Gandhi organized a group of stretcher-bearers who served on the front line. During World War I he recruited Indians for the war effort, and not just volunteers for the Ambulance Corps.

Gandhi's political approach, Satyagraha, including these eight principles, was presented in an article by Janis and Katz:

1. Refraining from any form of verbal or overt violence toward members of the rival group

2. Openly admitting to the rival group one's plans and intentions

3. Refraining from any action that will have the effect of humiliating the rival group

4. Making visible sacrifices for one's cause

5. Maintaining a consistent and persistent set of positive activities which are explicit (though partial) realizations of the group's objectives

6. Attempting to initiate direct personal interaction with members of the rival group

7. Adopting a consistent attitude of trust toward the rival group and taking overt actions which demonstrate that one is, in fact, willing to act upon this attitude

8. Attempting to achieve a high degree of empathy with respect to the motives, affects, expectations, and attitudes of members of the rival group. (1959: 85-100)

Let us look to the above eight aspects of Satyagraha that illustrate his nonviolent approach to conflict. All of them, with the exception of the fourth, specify not only nonviolent interaction with a rival group, but also the kind of interaction that points in an evolutionary direction. Emotions, such as humiliation (3) and trust (7), are also involved.

The power of one's passionate emotional commitment is well illustrated by one of Gandhi's volunteers when he and others were marching to occupy the salt depots in Dharsan in response to the salt tax that the British had initiated. Here they were required to be completely non-violent. An American journalist, Negley Farson, recorded an incident in which a Sikh, blood-soaked from the assault of a police sergeant, fell under heavy blows which he refused to deflect:

> He gave us a bloody grin and stood up to receive some more...[The police sergeant] was so sweaty from his exertions that his Sam Browne had stained his white tunic. I watched him with my heart in my mouth. He drew back his arm for a final swing – and then he dropped his hands down by his side. "It's no use," he said, turning to me with half an apologetic grin. "You can't hit a bugger when he stands up to you like that!" He gave the Sikh a mock salute and walked off (Quoted in Bondurant, op. cit., 96).

Publication of such stories reached the British public, putting increasing political pressure on the British government to repeal the salt tax. After many such acts of civil disobedience coupled with continuing pressure from the British public, the way was prepared for India being granted independence.

Given the Nazi and Japanese threats during World War II, Gandhi's Congress party did not push for independence immediately. But it was finally granted after the war in August, 1947. India continued its cultural and trade ties with Britain but gained control over its foreign policy and no longer was occupied by a British military force.

Gandhi's Eastern orientation helped him to focus on his own destiny, by contrast with the Western outward orientation. Yet that did not prevent him from interaction with others, convincing millions of Indians to join him in the struggle for independence.

Instead of remaining downtrodden as the result of the numerous acts of hatred that he suffered because his skin was not white, he converted those experiences into a deep awareness of a problem that he devoted his life to: India's lack of independence from Britain. As a result, he developed the emotional strength to persist in his Satyagraha or political battle for justice. Recall President Calvin Coolidge's belief: "Persistence and determination are omnipotent. The slogan 'press on' has solved and always will solve the problems of the human race."

...

A story of Tom Savage's experiences as a sheriff's deputy can help us to understand more fully the enormous negative impact of our present way of life on every single one of us. All of us have our dreams. However, some of those dreams, because of what we have seen and experienced, come to us as nightmares. Such was the reality for Tom, who, with apologies to Perry Mason, shares with us what he refers to as "the Case of the K-9 Disaster":

> To help develop a more trusting rapport between the police and children, the Officer Friendly Program had been established. This involved sending uniformed officers and deputies out to local schools, often bringing a patrol car, a mounted horse unit, and especially exciting, a fly-in by the sheriff's helicopter. Another favorite, an encounter with a police dog, a K-9 unit.
>
> I was scheduled to bring a K-9 unit to Gocio Elementary School, to visit Miss Bentley's third grade class, but the night before, a kid had gone

missing at our Myakka State Park, and all K-9 units were searching for the lost child.

What to do? I suddenly remembered a family just down the street from my apartment that owned a big seventeen-year-old German Shepherd who, due to old age, just slept most of the time, kind of smelled for lack of a regular bath, but who, once on his feet, looked great. Could I borrow him for the morning? "Yes," the owner said, "I could."

With Ranger, the dog's name, sitting beside me in the front seat, we raced out to the school to do our program. I decided to rename Ranger, giving him Roy Roger's dog's name, "Bullet." That would impress the kids.

Arriving at ten o'clock, the appointed time for our scheduled presentation, Ranger, er, Bullet, wearing his borrowed K-9 jacket, entered Miss Bentley's classroom, greeted by great applause.

Bringing Bullet to the front of the class, I commanded him to leap onto the teacher's desk. His front paws made it, but lacking any more strength, I had to lift his rear end up to complete the task. More applause.

For any program, first impressions are very important. Bullet certainly made his. Lifting a left hind leg, he sent a yellow stream of stress-reducing joy juice all over Miss Bentley's neatly arranged desk books. This, I now tried to explain to a completely enthralled class, was Bullet's way of marking the starting point of his investigation. More applause. Miss Bentley was not amused!

"Who will volunteer to take Bullet outside the classroom, so we can have him return to show us how he does a search for drugs?" David said he would, and during the absence of David and Bullet, I gave a short talk on "Just say no to drugs."

"Now, who will hide this bag of drugs (the supposed drugs were actually dog yummies to help the dog find them) in a desk?" Sarah put the bag in her desk. Mary Lou was sent out to bring back David and Bullet into the classroom.

Both were gone. Bullet had decided to just go for a walk, with David following him, assuming Bullet was indeed searching for hidden drugs. So, it took ten minutes to locate and return them both.

Once again, I had to make up an explanation for Bullet's behavior. "Bullet has now established a perimeter," not having a clue about what that was supposed to accomplish. Fortunately, no one asked.

Back in the classroom, Bullet began his drug search, row by row, desk by desk. A hush fell over the class as Bullet came up to Sarah's desk, but he proceeded to just walk on by. Evidently, age had compromised his sense of smell, including his own body's B.O.

I told Sarah to pretend there was another gang member in the class, and to toss the drugs to him, which she did. Bullet missed that act as well. It could have been a thrown football, and his bad vision would have taken no notice.

Another explanation was necessary. "As you can see, kids, Bullet is pretending not to observe these actions. Why? He's building a list of suspects!"

Finally, one student had the balls to state the obvious. From the back of the class, Billy Evans yelled out, "This is the dumbest dog I've ever seen."

"Dumb as a clever fox," I defensively shouted back. This foolish response was so ambiguous that a confused Billy was stunned into a profound silence.

I had rationalized bringing a fake K-9 to my presentation because he was to be no more than a prop, which was no big deal.

No big deal? The problem was that this prop was in fact a fraud. As the fraud started making more and more mistakes, I was forced to make up excuses for his behavior.

Understand, the word "excuses" here is merely a euphemism for Deputy Pinocchio's nose growing longer and longer because of his lies.

What a marvelous upright moral example for a man of the cloth, an officer of the law, to be telling lies to little and trusting kids. As Oliver Hardy used to tell Stan Laurel, "What a fine mess this is!"

With my program and me beginning to die, a kid, little Billy Evans, was nailing the coffin lid shut, telling everyone that the Emperor indeed has no clothes, and that this WAS the dumbest dog he had ever seen.

Defensively, I must add that Bullet wasn't dumb. He was just too old.

It was obvious to me that I now needed to bring this fiasco to an abrupt end.

Well, kids, our time is up, and Ranger and I have to leave. Again, Billy spoke up. "Who is Ranger?"
Oops. Wrong dog name. What to say? What to do?

Kids, I'm afraid I let slip a secret I shouldn't have told you. Ranger is the undercover name for Bullet. You must promise never to share this information with anyone. (Kids love secrets.) Please raise your hands to promise not to tell. All hands went up, except one. Billy wasn't buying it. His rebellion proved he would not be a dupe.

At that point, my nightmare would end. I'd wake up remembering that whole fiasco, trying only to forget.

How could I have set myself up to be the very thing I criticized others of being? I, too, had become a messenger of untruths with false facts, just trying to save face. I wanted to blame that dumb dog, Ranger, for my disgrace, but who went out and got him in the first place?

I received the usual "Thank you" letters from the students a few weeks later. All were complimentary. All except one. Billy had written, mocking the program warning children to beware of strangers. His letter read, "Stranger danger, Ranger stranger." Billy had exposed the deception. He would make a good cop as an adult.

Just like Tom, we all experience failures as well as successes. But we can learn from our negative experiences, as Tom did with his ability to unashamedly remind himself of just how much he had succeeded in betraying his own ideals. Instead of blaming ourselves, we can come to realize the enormous power of the forces in society that work against us.

…

Here is a success story to balance Tom's experience of a past failure. It centers on Astrid Cruz, a friend who has no Ph.D. and no Nobel Prize. She is not even a CEO. Born in Colombia, she is even a member of a minority group, a Latin-American. Yet she illustrates how people in general can learn to develop personal productivity.

At the age of twelve she read Richard Bach's book, *Jonathan Livingston Seagull*, and that changed her life, just as my own auditing of C. Wright Mills' class at Columbia changed my life.

The book tells the story of a seagull who is bored by daily squabbles over food and becomes seized by a passion for learning everything he can about flying. Although other seagulls turned their backs on him for his failure to conform to their way of life, that didn't stop him from experimenting with exhilarating challenges of daring aerial feats. And he continued experimenting throughout his life, for he saw no limit to his potentials.

Astrid's dream was to learn to become a special kind of photographer, someone able to help people see their own beauty and feel their own potential as human beings, thus learning to see themselves with different eyes.

After many years working in the medical field helping to support her children following a marriage that didn't work out, a second marriage to a part-time photographer finally enabled her to move closer to her dream. Finally, she and her husband opened their own photography studio. She has been able to leave her medical work and is now working full time in the studio, learning with her husband's help to move toward her dream.

I was there at the opening of the studio, where she gave a short talk about her vision. She said that people very often don't see themselves in very positive ways, but that they can learn to change that negative perspective with the aid of photography. Then she selected someone for a photographic makeover with the aid of a grooming specialist working with her and her husband. The result was absolutely unbelievable. I saw the magazine covers that they produced in their studio, and I viewed people who were clearly enjoying themselves and who looked supremely confident.

What Astrid illustrates is that there are many paths that can lead to personal and world evolution. Every single human being on the planet has unique experiences that apparently point in quite different directions. Yet all of those directions—whether raising children to open up to their potentials, working as a photographer, punching the time clock as an employee in a factory, or serving as a Justice of the U.S. Supreme Court—have in common their potential for moving one toward journeying on the yellow brick road of personal and world evolution.

No matter where we find ourselves in the world, even if our circumstances are very difficult ones, we can learn to find that yellow brick road. This is not the same as moving from rags to riches. Rather, it is moving toward a life before death.

...

Although we ordinarily think of productivity purely in economic terms, our idea of "personal productivity" extends far more widely, including the field of education.

Dr. Larry Thompson, President of Ringling College of Art and Design in Sarasota, Florida, gives us some insight into the "educational productivity" that is presently lacking in our school systems, and what can and should be done about it:

> In a study conducted by IBM, leaders of business organizations throughout the world were asked to identify the top leadership skills needed for future success.

> Of all the traits listed, the number one answer was—you guessed it—creativity!...I believe that everyone is creative. Everyone. We, as human beings, are born creative. Just look at children at play. They play by making up games and by turning whatever objects are available into toys to play with...

To put it bluntly, the problem is that too often we—we as a society—do our best to eliminate that natural creative tendency. We teach children to think alike, and to avoid the risks of failure that come with creativity. It happens in schools; it happens at work; and it happens in life itself (Thompson, 2017: B1, B6).

Thompson's idea that every single one of us is born creative brings to mind the difference between the sight of young children at play and us adults in our work cubicles within some large corporation. Where is emotional expression to be found?

With those children, and certainly not in those cubicles. For we adults have learned at school, at work, and everywhere else to get rid of any passionate emotional commitment that those children are expressing at play. Yet such emotional expression can become the basis for commitment to continue to develop oneself. It is that development which can yield creative solutions to problems of all kinds.

Tom recalls his effort to create just such a situation:

A traffic stop (you don't know who is in the vehicle, or if he is armed) and a domestic disturbance call (they're usually drunk or on drugs) are two of the most dangerous situations one can be dispatched to resolve.

A fighting couple had been reported to the Sheriff's Department, and when I arrived, the drunken husband was smashing all of the apartment's furniture, and he was currently holding a portable TV over his head, about to destroy it, while his drunken wife was yelling for me to "shoot'im, shoot'im."

I said, "OK, what's going on?" And they said in unison, "We want a divorce." And I said, "OK, you want a divorce. Raise your right hands. By the authority invested in me by the State of Florida and the Governor, I hereby declare that you are divorced. If I have to come back tonight, I will re-marry both of you. Do you understand these terms?" They said they did. We all shook hands, and I didn't have to go back again anytime during my eight-hour shift.

Here is an example of the power of genuine interaction for solving problems, for Tom listened and understood exactly what the couple wanted. Given their inebriated state, it didn't take much to convince them that he had the authority to grant their wish.

...

Tom tells us of yet another problem: There is the painful and difficult task of officers delivering a notification of the death of a spouse, usually the result of an unexpected heart attack or car accident. Because of his ministerial background, he was asked by an official of the Law Enforcement Academy to go up in front of the recruit class and demonstrate just how to deliver this message.

Pretending to knock on a door, he said, "Widow Johnson?" It got a laugh, but everyone knows how difficult the scene would be. Grown women have fainted on the spot, and he even had that personal experience. Men expressed anger and outrage that an irresponsible drunk driver had killed a family member. The words of an officer, and just how they are delivered, matter a great deal.

It is here that an officer's personal productivity counts. For example, one's emotional development can enable one to have empathy for the situation of others, and to express genuine concern rather than interact with no expression of personal feelings.

One of the most difficult situations that Tom faced, occurred after informing a wife that her husband had died. Tom was shocked when she responded to the news by saying, "Well, his brother is not going to get the tools in our garage."

...

Here is another of Tom's stories of actions that can succeed in solving problems:

> A friend of mine confessed that he saw no importance or value in the world of art. I said that this was very interesting, because art had become central to my own life.
>
> I noticed that my friend had recently purchased a new truck. "How is it," I asked, "that you chose that particular truck? After all, they all have the same basic performance package under the hood."
>
> "Well," he said, "I kind of liked the way it looked."
>
> "You mean, its design. That's art," I noted. "What you see means a great deal regarding how you feel. And you are obviously quite proud about how your truck looks."
>
> "You're right," the friend admitted. "It looks great!"

Tom's response links art to feelings or emotions. His story illustrates the idea that we all are interested in art at least to some extent, for we all express our emotions somewhat. Yet we can all learn to do much better.

We might also note that the idea of Tom's friend that he was not interested in art got in the way of his learning to appreciate art, and thus to express his emotions more fully. His attitude about art placed him in an unrealistic fantasy world. Yet Tom succeeded in making visible what had previously been invisible to his friend, enabling him to break out of his fantasy world into the world of reality.

...

Educational productivity can occur everywhere and not just in school buildings. Tom tells us a story about his experiences as a camp counselor:

> As a camp counselor, you really do care for these campers, and everyone appreciates being noticed and respected. Unfortunately, God, for reasons unknown and unclear, has not made all of us equal in terms of looks or ability. So it is hard not to praise and champion those who do excel. Even more difficult not to condemn or jump on those youth who seem to fail to recognize their own full potential, content on acting more like clowns than winners.
>
> Such was the conversation we counselors were having, evaluating various kids under our care, when suddenly a rather well developed weenie was stuck out through a knothole from inside one of the camp cabins.
>
> As leaders, we all looked at one another, then yelled out together, "June Bug Prentis Moore, get your ass out here, front and center." We didn't even have to see the culprit. Only he would have been so stupidly brave.
>
> "Just what do you think you were doing?" we barked. "Pissing," was the honest reply. "But through a knothole?"
>
> "Better than in the cabin. The bathroom is too far up the hill, and I had to go."
>
> This conversation was going in no positive direction. He had done wrong, but I must confess, inwardly all of us as leaders were laughing our heads off.
>
> "OK, June Bug. Help us out here. What have you learned from all of this?"
>
> "To make sure the coast is clear" was his answer.
>
> Checkmate. He had won. A born leader if ever there was one, definitely fit for a later vocation in politics or law.

June Bug is by no means cowed by all of the counselors put together, for he doesn't back down a single inch from what he has done. His self-confidence is most apparent as he calls a spade a spade. He stands out from all of the other campers, for only he would have been so stupidly brave.

Never mind June Bug's sticking his weenie in a knothole to relieve himself on camp grounds. He has learned to interact with the counselors on an equal footing rather than bow down to them while full of emotions like fear and guilt. That is exactly the learning that educators should encourage, just as those counselors did not come down hard on June Bug for what he had done.

Contrast the behavior of those counselors with Paolo Freire's analysis of education: "The teacher teaches and the students are taught. The teacher knows everything and the students know nothing. The teacher thinks and the students are thought about. The teacher talks and the students listen—meekly."

...

Our journey for self-discovery is nearing its end, granting that this journey can become much of the basis for a lifetime journey that follows it.

Much of this book centers on the personal experiences of Bernie Phillips and Tom Savage, granting that the assistance of Andy Plotkin, Neil Weiss and Max Spitzer was absolutely invaluable.

We five authors have presented our distinct insights throughout this book. Now, however, the time has come for the two authors who have had the most to say throughout these pages—Bernie Phillips, a scholar, and Tom Savage, a preacher—to reveal more of themselves.

THE SCHOLAR'S TALE

How is the reader to possibly apply our ideas to his or her own personal situation so as to move toward an ever more meaningful life as well as toward an increasing ability to help solve world problems?

Given a lifetime of failing to see the invisible forces that shape us, how can we open our eyes to them?

Is it really possible to pay attention to one's own personal development in a world that has succeeded in taking us away from any focus on ourselves?

If we've never learned to free ourselves from abject conformity to the rules of the bureaucratic game, how can we proceed to break those bonds and escape from prison?

And what about world problems, which appear to be increasingly threatening, with no way in sight of solving them?

Where are the social scientists who are responsible for figuring out what is wrong and how to make it right?

How can we possibly confront the fact that we are now two minutes to Midnight, according to 15 Nobel Laureates and others who have studied nuclear, biological and chemical dangers coupled with climate change and many others?

It is now, at the conclusion of this book, that I will put forward my optimistic view of our future.

But this is not simply another personal story—we've heard so many—about how an individual somehow, after terrible adversity, managed to come out on top. Those stories are important, for in these times we need all the encouragement we can get.

My favorite story is about the 19th-Century poet William Ernest Henley.

He was diagnosed with tubercular arthritis at the age of 12, and he suffered years of pain in addition to growing up within an impoverished family. His medical condition required the amputation of one of his legs. When told that his other leg would also require amputation, he refused, seeking the help of a distinguished surgeon who managed to save it after multiple operations. While recovering he was moved to write Invictus:

> Out of the night that covers
> me, Black as the pit from
> pole to pole, I thank whatever
> gods may be
> For my unconquerable soul.
>
> In the fell clutch of circumstance
> I have not winced nor cried
> aloud. Under the
> bludgeonings of chance
> My head is bloody but unbowed.
>
> Beyond this place of wrath and
> tears Looms but the Horror of
> the shade, And yet the measure
> of the years Finds, and shall
> find me, unafraid.
>
> It matters not how straight the gate,
> How charged with punishments the scroll,
> I am the master of my fate:
> I am the captain of my soul. (Quoted in Knowles, op. cit., 381/13, 14)

"Invictus," Latin for "unconquered," is a poem that inspired Nelson Mandela, former President of South Africa, during the twenty-seven years he spent in a prison on Robben Island. The poem also helped Franklin D. Roosevelt continue with his political career after contracting a paralytic disease at the age of 39. During the early years of World War II when Britain faced the probability of invasion by the Nazi war machine, Winston Churchill's speech to the House of Commons paraphrased the poem's last two lines: "We are still masters of our fate. We still are captains of our souls."

Henley's vision can equally encourage the rest of us. Granting "the night that covers" us, given "the bludgeonings of chance," and accounting for "the Horror of the shade," every single one of us has every right to claim: "I am the captain of my soul."

In our present time we certainly need such inspiration. But we need more than that. We need to understand how we can confront effectively our double crisis. How are we to actually achieve a truly meaningful life before we arrive at our deathbed?

Is it really possible for us to help solve the deepening problems of the modern world?

What we require is the ability to build on knowledge and understanding from sociology, psychology, anthropology, economics, political science, and history.

In addition to emotional commitment, we need intellectual understanding. Following the pendulum metaphor for the scientific method, it is both of these forces that are required to make progress on our personal and world problems, and then to keep making further progress.

As one illustration, recall that Jane Addams—who wrote about democracy as a sentiment, a creed, and a rule of living—also wrote that "the cure for the ills of democracy is more democracy." But exactly what would be the nature of "more democracy"?

Following Corey Dolgon's *Kill It to Save It: An Autopsy of Capitalism's Triumph over Democracy* (2017), will the death of capitalism—accompanied by ending the worldwide increasing gap between the rich and the poor—yield what Addams called for?

Alternatively, will Thomas Piketty's *Capital in the Twenty-First Century* (2014)—with its call for a progressive income tax that redistributes income from the rich to the poor—be the answer that we need?

Perhaps, instead, among other things we need Robert B. Reich's *Saving Capitalism For the Many, Not the Few* (2016)—calling for increasing the power of unions so that a redistribution is not required.

Perhaps, instead, we need what John Dewey called for, where "the central mission of government, business, education, religion, and the family should be to educate every individual into the full stature of his possibility" (1920/1948: 186).

Perhaps, instead, we also need the increasing "personal productivity" in all aspects of life that is the product of that kind of education.

We do not pretend that we have presented a thorough economic analysis in this book that can follow up on Addams' vision of achieving more democracy. Yet unlike Dolgon, our own vision by no means requires the death of capitalism.

The books by both Piketty and Reich do succeed in adding to our understanding of how the market works and how to develop a more equitable economy. Yet neither one dips deeply into the overall organization of society, and not just the market. They illustrate the very best work of our specialized world, yet we need in addition the interdisciplinary approach that our own book represents.

Such a direction must open up the incredible potential of each one of us to continue to develop intellectually, emotionally, and in our ability to solve problems with absolutely no limit as to how far we can go.

Our direction calls for an education that will enable us to release that potential so that we can gain not only more democracy. We must also achieve a more meaningful life along with the ability to solve our increasingly threatening problems.

I did not suffer anything like Henley's experiences of terrible pain. Nor did I contract polio and the paralysis that followed, as did Roosevelt. Neither was I a victim of Nazi bombings, as was Churchill and others throughout the British Isles. But my tale nevertheless has that same sense of urgency.

I look far back in my personal history to the year 1940 when I was a nine-year-old elementary school student at Public School 61 in the Bronx at the beginning of World War II. I was the teacher's pet, for I was an A student, and in the 3rd grade Mrs. Israel appointed me Editor-in-Chief of the 3B News. We sold it for three cents a copy with visions of enormous sales. But the only buyers were our parents. So our meager proceeds were all we could give to the Red Cross.

But on the playground during recess it was an entirely different story for me. I was bullied both mentally and physically by some of my classmates. It was not just a question of not being chosen for participation in basketball and baseball. It was also being called names, such as "teacher's pet," "momma's boy," "asshole" and "shitface." And I was even shoved and thrown on the ground.

Also, I was unable to defend myself, in part because I really was a momma's boy. I was in fact babied by my mother, who was an immigrant from Romania and didn't understand the importance of my learning to demonstrate physical strength and fearlessness on the playground and elsewhere.

These experiences on the playground, repeated throughout my entire elementary school career, pushed me away from developing personal friendships and toward a narrow focus on doing well academically. They also pushed me away from developing any ability to express my emotions. I learned to repress or bury my feelings of fear and shame, and I felt guilty about my inability to learn how to change my deep sense of isolation.

Most important, that shame, guilt and fear illustrated the fact that I blamed myself for what had happened on the elementary-school playground. I also blamed myself for my experiencing these negative emotions, as well as for my deep sense of isolation. My self-image took a beating, and I developed little self-confidence. As I grew up, as well as throughout my later life, I tried and tried to figure out how to develop more confidence. But I never escaped from my deep feelings of shame, guilt, and fear. Overall, I felt that my problems were my own fault. This prevented me from developing feelings of self-acceptance and self-confidence, a very far cry from my empowerment.

Yet those negative feelings, granting that they persisted throughout much of my life, did not prove to be terminal. For throughout my academic career I gradually moved away from them as I continued to express myself in a series of books.

By far the greatest turning point came when I finally left the academic world. Much like Helen Keller's experience when she learned the word for her experience with water, that departure "awakened my soul, gave it light, hope, set it free!" For I was no longer under the thumb of an organization that provided the employment that I needed. And my books had pointed a way for me to move away from the shackles of conformity to hierarchies and a narrow intellectual orientation.

The big change in my life came when I audited a class with C. Wright Mills at Columbia. I was a shy boy, not tall in stature, with little cultural background and less confidence, who commuted to college from the East Bronx.

Mills would arrive at Columbia on his motorcycle, wearing a coonskin hat with its tail waving in the breeze. On the fourth floor of Hamilton Hall, we students crowded around the windows, alerted by the enormous sound that he deliberately made.

Mills was tall and wide, and roared in the classroom. He was angry about society's failure to deal with fundamental problems, angry with his sociological colleagues who shied away from trying to solve them, and angry at institutions like Columbia that tolerated such behavior.

He became my ideal, a Superman who appeared to have the answers to what society needed. And also what I needed, if only I could somehow gain at least a tiny bit of his incredible self-confidence.

Mills had not yet written his most famous book, The Sociological Imagination (1959). But nevertheless he pointed his students in a direction that opposed the increasing specialization throughout the social sciences.

Throughout my academic career I pursued that interdisciplinary direction. But without his charisma, it was not an easy road for me to follow. I was still the same timid and relatively isolated individual that I had been earlier, only carrying more and more academic credentials.

I recall a time, after two years working on a research project in the University of North Carolina's School of Public Health, that I found myself on a plane headed for a job interview at the Champagne-Urbana campus of the University of Illinois. My aim was to secure a position in the school's Department of Sociology, which would have much higher status in my field than being a researcher outside of a sociology department.

I soon realized that, while my seat was near the front of the plane, someone who looked like Mills had a seat in the back. Yet I was too shy to walk up to the Great Man to introduce myself. Later, I learned that it was in fact Mills, for he had come to deliver a lecture on his latest book, The Causes of World War III (1958).

I will not easily forget what I had thought was my great achievement. After some five years of work on the data that I'd collected in that project at North Carolina, I'd finally submitted an article based on my findings. Our research group had studied the forces that influence medical students to make their choices of medical specialties. The U.S. Public Service had financed the project because of its interest in learning why so few medical students chose public health as a career.

The data I'd been working with was based on detailed questionnaires completed by several thousand medical students throughout the country. It was quite a trove of information, for it included over a hundred pieces of data about each medical student in the study.

My aim was to demonstrate that it is possible, with enough information about a given person, to go far beyond the usual minimal understanding of why anyone makes any given choice, not just a medical student's choice of a specialty. For published social science studies, focused on the behavior of groups, almost invariably were based on very little data on any given individual. That situation was in turn largely based on social scientists' focus on social structure, and not on personality structure.

I had managed to figure out how to integrate all of the information about any given student in the study with the aid of a very simple mathematical model. As a result, I was able to predict quite accurately, on the basis of a student's goals and beliefs, just which specialty he or she actually preferred. Those predictions far exceeded in their accuracy the results of any publications about individual choices that I'd ever read.

Yet when I submitted my article, "Expected Value Deprivation and Occupational Preference," to Sociometry—a leading journal in social psychology— reviewers rejected it because my mathematical model was unique, not conforming to models that had previously been published.

I recall being very depressed for perhaps a week. But then I became angry about what I believed was the failure of those reviewers to act in a truly scientific fashion. I re-submitted my manuscript with a detailed argument for its publication, and—lo and behold—it was finally accepted and soon published (1964).

At that point I waited breathlessly for responses from my social science colleagues, correspondence commenting on my achievement. Alas, absolutely none was forthcoming.

Over the years after that experience, I attempted in many ways to move my social science colleagues in the direction of paying attention to the individual. I founded two book series focused on advancing the sociological imagination. I also founded "The Sociological Imagination Group," which had annual research meetings that resulted in three edited volumes (Phillips, Kincaid and Scheff, eds., 2002; Phillips, ed., 2007; Knottnerus and Phillips, eds. 2009).

Yet these efforts failed to change social science's march toward ever further specialization that excluded attention to the full breadth of the individual human being.

But I've not given up in my efforts with my colleagues, as illustrated by my just-published article in Contemporary Sociology, "Sociology's Next Steps?" (2019).

What started me on my present path some seven years ago was an e-mail from Andy Plotkin, my former doctoral student at Boston University. He wanted to initiate a new school based on an interdisciplinary approach to the social sciences. I decided to join him.

After several years we realized that we were not in a financial position to inaugurate a school, so our idea morphed into developing this book. Later, we were joined by Neil Weiss, one of Andy's colleagues. Still later, one of Andy's students, Max Spitzer, became interested in working with us.

Yet we were all limited by our academic orientation. Purely by accident, I met Tom Savage while we were both waiting for Barnes & Noble to open its doors. We immediately joined forces. Tom had become disappointed with both the ministry and his law-enforcement experiences, which had failed to find solutions for contemporary societal problems; and both of us had become equally disappointed by the failures of social scientists to do much better.

We found that by working together, joined by Plotkin, Weiss and Spitzer, we would achieve a breadth of perspective that could succeed in building on an extremely wide range of knowledge about human behavior. This could be an interdisciplinary approach that would pay close attention to the vast knowledge that had presently been accumulated.

As a result, we believed that we could accomplish what we'd all desired: a book that would succeed in actually confronting effectively our double crisis of personal meaningless and escalating world problems. Readers, this is the book you now hold in your hands.

Looking back at my personal journey, I see it as illustrating both the enormous power over us of our bureaucratic way of life, and also the incredible potential of the individual, in interaction with others, for opposing that power so as to move from our see-saw onto a stairway.

That had been achieved to a limited extent by the individuals cited in this book, by the students in the Levin experiment who compared their grades with their own previous grades, and by the industrial workers in Japan after World War II who adopted a kaizen or continuing-improvement mentality.

I've illustrated in these few pages my own journey, a very long-term process that is focused on confronting the problem of our double crisis. It is illustrated by the initial failure of the editors of Sociometry to publish my article, on the one hand, and my subsequent argument for its publication and achievement of that goal, on the other hand. Along with everyone else, I had experienced failures no less than successes. Also, in common with many others, I would not let those failures defeat me, but would follow them with efforts that finally overturned them. Those actions sometimes took years, as in the case of this book.

Yet these pages describe a path for all of us that is extremely short. Compare it to my lifelong experience of building on whatever I knew previously to emerge with a direction for any reader to confront any and all personal and world problems.

It is an education in personal productivity that builds on the basic tools that we humans have invented.

By so doing, we can pay attention to both the impact on us of our present way of life as well as the incredible potential of an alternative way of life.

We can also learn to tie any of our concrete actions in ordinary life to our vision of our own continuing improvement throughout life.

Every single one of us has different experiences from one situation to the next. By linking our own unique experiences to that vision, we can actually move toward fulfilling that ideal. This is an exceedingly democratic approach, by contrast with requiring everyone to adopt it. It is not a one-size-fits-all strategy.

Also, we can learn to take only one step at a time so as to be most realistic about our continuing journey.

As a result, we can learn to continually shorten the very long periods that I had undergone that were required to swing my pendulum back and forth. We can, as a result, continue to speed up the process of personal evolution that can accelerate the development of our own personal productivity.

Readers will most likely remember this saying: "For want of a nail the shoe was lost. For want of a shoe the horse was lost. For want of a horse the rider was lost. For want of a rider the battle was lost. For want of the battle the war was lost. For want of the war the nation was lost. And all for the want of a horseshoe nail."

The poet William Blake captured the significance of this saying when he wrote, "He who would do good to another, must do it in minute particulars." Here is an example of accentuating the positive rather than the negative:

> Because I was angry at school shootings, I became more passionate.
> Because I became more passionate, I wrote a letter to the editor.
> Because I wrote a letter to the editor, I developed a following on social media.
> Having developed a following on social media I ran for Congress. Having run for Congress, I was elected.
> Having been elected, I influenced social science research.
> Having influenced social science research, I initiated projects developing personal productivity.
> Having initiated projects developing personal productivity, some organizations improved the productivity of their workers.
> When some organizations developed the productivity of their workers, others followed suit.
> When other organizations followed suit, we succeeded in developing a more educational society.
> When we developed a more educational society, aggression and addiction became things of the past.
> And it all began because I was angry at school shootings.

Our own journey together is by no means over. It has just begun. For we plan to continue our efforts, for as long as it takes, to help solve that double crisis in which we all find ourselves.

> READER, WE HOPE OUR BOOK WILL INSPIRE YOU TO JOIN US. SHARE OUR OPTIMISM ABOUT THE INCREDIBLE POTENTIAL OF EVERY SINGLE HUMAN BEING, BASED ON THE FOURTEEN-BILLION-YEAR JOURNEY WE HAVE ALREADY TAKEN.
>
> SHARE OUR BELIEF IN OUR CAPACITY TO UNLOCK THE ENORMOUS POWER OF LANGUAGE AND THE SCIENTIFIC METHOD.
>
> SHARE OUR CONVICTION THAT EVERY ONE OF US CAN LEARN TO APPLY THESE TOOLS TO CONFRONT EVER MORE EFFECTIVELY OUR DOUBLE CRISIS OF MEANINGLESSNESS AND INCREASING WORLD PROBLEMS.

Looking to Tom's personal journey, he has been retired for over twenty years. Yet, even now at age 80, there occasionally come to mind haunting memories from experiences his two professional roles provided. He cannot forget the sorrow and sadness, the pain and suffering, the despair and death with which he had to deal.

As a minister, he was a teacher. As a law enforcement deputy, he had been a learner. Ranger and Billy had helped keep him humble. A Great Dane named Max had given him courage. A beach wedding, authority and command.

With a smile he remembers the number of people who encountered him as a cop, saying he had missed his calling. A uniform and badge couldn't hide compassion. He wasn't a cop pretending to be a minister. He was a minister displaying a sense of integrity that made him respected as a good cop.

When Tom met Bernard Phillips, and they began writing Creating Life Before Death, Tom had lost his faith in making a difference in the lives of others, let alone believing he could impact world problems.

Today, he doesn't ask, "What can I do?" He now understands that all of us, when engaged and empowered, can, will and must make a difference.

SO, LET US ALL ROLL UP OUR SLEEVES, AND GET THE MUCH NEEDED JOB DONE.

THE PREACHER'S TALE

Edgar Bergen was a wonderful story-teller who had to deal with a chagrined wooden-headed puppet, Charlie McCarthy, who reluctantly was his captive audience.

> **Bergen**: "Today, Charlie, I'm going to share with you a tale that took place over three thousand years ago."
> **Charlie**: "Oh, I'm sure this will be a goodie one!"
> **Bergen**: "Two great empires, the Greeks and the Trojans, found themselves at war, all started by the abduction of a famous woman called Helen of Troy."
> **Charlie**: "Why didn't they just give her back?"
> **Bergen**: "Now, for the Greeks, their champion fighter was Achilles. For the Trojans, their hero was Paris. Both were basically equal in strength and valor, with one notable exception. Achilles had been dunked in the river Stix, which made him immortal."
> **Charlie**: "The river, what?"
> **Bergen**: "Stix."
> **Charlie**: "Well, maybe at low tide, it just didn't smell all that good."
> **Bergen**: "No, Charlie. The name of the river was Stix. But, for Achilles, there had been a problem. In dunking him, his mother had held on to his heel, which didn't get the benefit of immortality. And history has referred to this reality as one's Achilles heel, which means a fatal flaw."
> **Charlie**: "Yes, I suppose that could be a problem."
> **Bergen**: "Now, Paris knew of this weakness, so he shot an arrow into Achilles' heel, and he died."
> **Charlie**: "And that's the last time he saw Paris."

Bergen: "So you see, Charlie, it's good to know that each of us, for different reasons, has a capacity for creativity, but also a potential flaw. Awareness of this fact should help guide a person in his or her choices. Do you understand?"

Charlie: "Yes, I do. What I don't understand is why you think these stories have anything to do with me."

Bergen: "Well, Charlie, life's lessons come to us through the trials and errors of experience. Tales of famous men and women help us learn from their successes and mistakes. This story in particular could help you become a better little boy."

Charlie: "Oh, I don't know. I always felt I was better off just ignoring your advice."

Poor Charlie! Satisfied to merely manipulate and trick all who know him. His sarcasm and flippant remarks merely betray a lack of taking his life seriously. And, as is so often the case, he ends up being the victim of his own poor choices.

Another revealing tale has been told regarding a rich merchant of Baghdad, who summoned forth his servant, saying, "I would dine with my friends this evening. Go to the market place and purchase the necessary provisions for our banquet." The servant bowed himself out of his master's presence, and hurried off to do his bidding.

But, in a short period of time he returned, shaking and trembling with great fear. "Master! Master," he cried out. "Please, you must help me. For I went to the market place as you commanded, and there I saw Death, and he made threatening gestures toward me. I know he has come to take me away. Do not allow this to be my Fate. Please help me to flee the city."

And his master, having great compassion for his faithful servant, provided him with his swiftest horse, and the poor man raced out of Baghdad, riding to the nearby city of Samarra.

Now, the more he thought about all that had transpired, the angrier the rich merchant became, for obviously there would be no party that night. So, dressing himself he marched up to the market place. Seeing Death, he approached him, saying, "How is it that you came to the market place this morning and made threatening gestures toward my servant?"

Death replied: "I! I did not make threatening gestures toward your servant. I was merely startled to see him here in Baghdad, for I have an appointment with him tonight in Samarra."

In John O'Hara's novel, Appointment in Samarra (1934), the author distinguishes between two ideas: Fate and Destiny. Fate is understood to be something we have little or no control over. However, the only Fate that I am willing to acknowledge is our human condition: we are born, we live, and we die.

Rich or poor, wise or foolish, all participate in, and no one escapes, this reality.

But, Destiny. Ah, Destiny. Here we do have choices. And having choices can make all the difference in the quality of our lives. Following existentialist ideas, our

Fate is to be "thrown into the world." Now, what choices do we make? Remember. Our choices become our destiny!

Think of the arena of time. What a difference to have been thrown into the world of the first century, versus the tenth, or our own century. And what of location? How different one's experiences to have been thrown into China, Africa, the Middle East, Europe, or the American continent. And what of condition? Imposing or diminutive stature? Wealth or poverty? Male or female? Servant or master? The list goes on.

But the challenge for each of us has been well captured in a Texas saying: "Rise above your raising." In other words, produce through a lifetime of learning a nobler vision than that provided by your present way of life, achieving a more dynamic and fuller life before death. For you can control your own Destiny, even if not your Fate.

...

Your authors have taken you on a journey from a 13.8 billion year beginning to the modern 21st Century, sharing the ideas and wisdom of writers and thinkers who have helped shape the world in which we live.

As a child, you enjoyed the freedom to create a place for self-discovery and fantasy to satisfy both personal needs and a sense of meaning. But, the adult must eventually leave this realm of safety in order to survive and succeed in the harsh realities of a less than perfect world.

In this book, we have encouraged and argued for a life-long study of human growth and development, remembering, of course, a viewpoint seeing all history as a process of selective remembrance. Millions of events and incidents, and for want of a recorder, billions of individuals have come and gone without any telling.

We have been blessed with a modern insightful perspective holding a healthy rejection of belief in the presumptive authority of the past. Today's empiricism, experimentation, rationalism, individualism, and skepticism about certainty have all helped us to understand that not only we, but ideas, too, change over a period of time. Today's thoughts challenge all relationships of power. This newer understanding asks less of how to go to heaven, and more of how the heavens go.

We live in an "Age of Doubt," but as Tennyson observed, "There lives more faith in honest doubt than in half the creeds." The cynic believes in nothing. The atheist at least "believes" there is no God.

In one of my favorite states, Texas, I have always enjoyed a sign which has God saying, "Don't make me come down there!" Pretty strong stuff!

It has been said that the gods didn't want humans to know the Truth, but didn't know where to hide it. Finally, they decided to hide it in humans themselves, because that is the last place where they would look for it.

The existentialist says, "Don't ask what the meaning of life is; ask what meaning we can give life." For one should in the end be more than a mere victim of genetics and environment.

We have our work cut out for us because human nature is not always predictable, coherent, or precise. The constants of our history seem to revolve around money, commerce, and conquest. Seeking a balance between structure and freedom, stability and change, is never an easy task.

Many are overwhelmed if they discover a new-found freedom. Now they fear having to make so many choices. So, they seek a misguided safety by deciding not to choose. Not choosing is a choice, which only allows others to step up to define and control them.

How paradoxical that our freedom is one of the most demanding of responsibilities. Albert Camus said, "Freedom is merely a chance to be better." Sartre tells us, "We are our choices," remembering that we are today because of the choices we made yesterday!

We should, therefore, choose to seek a better quality of life, willingly accepting the challenge of creating a nobler direction and purpose for our existence, recognizing that there is a big difference between really living and just existing.

So, let us rise above the mere maintenance issues of life—food, clothing, shelter, entertainment, and sex—all admittedly important, but not enough to answer life's questions about true meaning and significance. For life is a journey, and we should try to make it an adventure of limitless possibilities.

If you believe that you determine what life means, and that you may choose the values that are most important, then act on that belief. If you believe that you can or cannot win, you are right! It's your choice! Your authors hold that happiness is the result of zestful living. We invite you to join us in this quest, seeking to have a great life before your death.

Now, before you accuse us of being rather Pollyanna-type authors, let us emphatically state that "all is not well." We have a problem here! Yes, a problem! If not, then why have we written this book?

We authors use metaphors throughout the book to help explain more difficult concepts by likening them to something more familiar. Thus, we begin to define part of "the problem" by referring to a Doomsday Clock which writers say now stands at two minutes to Midnight, which could end civilization as we know it.

You, the readers, may well respond that history provides us with a long list of circumstantial problems and challenges. But this time it is different! Yes, we always have had conflicts and troubles, but never before have we witnessed the destructive power of modern atomic, biological and chemical weapons, and such unstable leaders willing to release madness. Here we have the Vietnam mentality of "We destroyed this village in order to save it."

After this first possibility of civilization's destruction comes our next problem. This vision of humankind's annihilation is evidently so horrible to even contemplate that it remains for most a practically "invisible crisis."

Another part of the problem consists of a failure to distinguish between outer and inner space. Too much focus centers on the former, where ignoring the latter causes us to fail to develop our full potential.

We need a noble vision to address these issues. We have noted multiple times that Proverbs 29:18 responds: "Where there is no vision, the people perish." And, your principal author's favorite Japanese proverb: "Vision without action is a daydream; action without vision is a nightmare."

We see that a person grows and changes over time, both physically and intellectually. This evolutionary development proves that change is both necessary and beneficial.

Finally, we assert that for a broader, richer understanding of our human condition, we need an interdisciplinary scientific methodology for effective action.

The various disciplines, such as biology, physics, chemistry, psychology, sociology, anthropology, literature, art, etc., need to be talking and sharing with one another. Unfortunately, this is seldom the case, resulting in a failure to see the "Big Picture." What should we do? First, independent creativity must replace standardized procedures.

Second, reject a hierarchy of narrow specialties that compromise effective action.

Third, recognize that a close-minded bureaucratic mentality, stressing conformity over innovation, is causing our social problems, not solving them.

Fourth, admit that the unexamined life is not worth living.

Fifth, join Isaac Newton by showing our debt to the past as we continue to stand on the shoulders of giants.

Sixth, understand the old saying that as we think, so we feel, and later take action. We call this "head," "heart" and "hand."

Seventh, appreciate that competition and cooperation are mutually beneficial. Eighth, acknowledge that ideas should enable rather than restrict.

Ninth, see that our problems must be resolved, not just debated and discussed. Tenth, admit that time is running out for solving humankind's problems. Eleventh, it is inappropriate to judge a race, nation, or group by its least worthy members.

Twelfth, agree with William James, who instructs us "to act as if what we plan to do will make a difference."

Thomas Huxley, too, wrote, "The great end of life is not knowledge but action."

Have we not learned that custom and convention often are inseparable from ignorance and hypocrisy?

We know through personal experience that the idea of the good, beautiful, and true will not be understood in the same way tomorrow. We know language is civilization's gift. However, because of different definitions and understandings, words and concepts can either enable or restrict.

Science supposedly deals in facts, the humanities in values. But the words "atoms," "earth," and "universe" all had different meanings in the 19th Century. The reality of atoms was hotly debated. As for the earth, no one had even heard of plate tectonics. The universe was the Milky Way, other galaxies being unknown. Is the universe one of purpose and order, or chance and chaos? And, yes, your answer matters.

The chief aim of Hindu and Buddhist thought is to unveil the hidden, not describe the visible world. The East seeks contemplation; the West analysis. Each has something to teach and offer the other.

The facts of life suggest that we are caught between a vanished past and an unknown future.

All should seek to become masters of our lives, not slaves to our circumstances. Robert M. Pirsig's book, Zen and the Art of Motorcycle Maintenance (1974), urges that if we are unable to do great things, do small things in a great way. In other words, it's not what you do, but how you do it.

Today, we reject the new twenty-first century moral climate, suggesting that everything is acceptable, and no one is accountable.

We should rejoice when Winnie-the-Pooh's Christopher Robin says, "You are braver than you believe, stronger than you seem, and smarter than you think." Frank Baum, the author of The Wizard of Oz and The Land of Oz, had his Wizard give much the same advice to the Scarecrow, the Tin Man, and the Cowardly Lion. The

Beatle George Harrison warns, "If you don't know where you are going, any road will take you there."

Edith Barr Dunn, a beautiful lady in Sarasota Florida now passed, said, "It's nice to be important, but it's more important to be nice." She helped us all to appreciate that what you think becomes your world.

Edith's claim to fame came when she was an owner/manager of a local restaurant when, one morning, who should bounce in but none other than Elvis Presley, who was performing that night in Sarasota. Not being an overwhelmed and screaming teenager, she later told reporters that Mr. Presley had been very nice and polite. She could have had the decency to have at least fainted on the spot.

Cicero told us that it was a great injustice to sit around doing nothing when others were out doing wrong. Both Edith and Cicero seem to be saying that when you retire, try to inspire before you expire. Always be open to new ideas. Be curious to investigate and independent in your thinking. Try to remember that self-control begins and ends with thought control.

It has, as I approach the end of my life, been hard for me to accept the reality that life has offered no final answers. But I celebrate the fact that it provided many choices. Don't wait until the end of your life to consider what was really most important for you.

Are you in the bleachers, watching others play the game of life? Get up. Get started. Be involved. Each of us has the power to reinvent himself or herself. Learn from the past, not just continue to live it.

Finally, I don't want to be an Aladdin. No life should be limited to just three wishes.

But, let this be an affirmation gifting future generation with our knowledge, experiences, and wisdom.

Fact: The mind tends to wander! Present experiences are ignored in favor of past recollections, filled with mixed memories of people and events. Remembering negative images are the mind's way of warning us of potential dangers. It was supposed to have been a thinking system for survival.

Unfortunately, this mental review usually dwells on our own mistakes and failures. The result becomes the creation of an emotional state too often focused on sadness, regrets, fears, ending in a quasi-state of depression.

The goal of this book has been to stop this negative process, changing supposed problems into liberating challenges.

Each of us has to deal with everyday difficulties. As a result, daily stress is a modern commonplace. Acceptance of this fact is paramount. Recognition that your body can be in one place, and your mind in another, is the beginning of awareness and wisdom!

Change and loss are inevitable. This produces our condition of unhappiness. Why do we bother comparing ourselves with others? Fifty percent of the people will not like us because they are not like us. This is due to different biases and prejudices, plus conflicting beliefs found in the geography of cultures.

The world is seldom what we wish it were. But our judgments should not always be believed. Automatic reactions can compromise rather than enable.

If we seek to be energized, we need to be totally engaged in life. We both compete and cooperate in order to survive.

When we start to recognize the processes that bring distress, we should stop our own wandering minds, and gain personal control.

Let's concentrate on the positive, make use of the immediate moment, and enjoy a new sense of renewal.

The human animal was created to survive, not to be happy. Is it any wonder most of our life issues involve stress related disorders? Living in today's fast-paced world, what we have to face is not always our fault. But we can control our responses to the world's demands.

The reward—a new and more creative and productive life.

There is no time like the present, and now is the time for us to act. Our human condition has provided us with a birth, a life, and a death. We've had our moments in the sun, yet know all tales finally reach THE END.

There is no time like the present, and now is the time for us to act. Our human condition has provided us with a birth, a life, and a death. We've had our moments in the sun, yet know all tales finally reach THE END.

In the Tree of Life, how like a leaf our lives have been. As my poem, "The Leaf," says,

> Here am I
> Once supple, smooth, alive
> Now rigid, course, dying
> Soon to drift quietly to the ground where expectant seedlings
> Greedily await my life-giving death. Those gentle breezes who
> Yesterday fondly caressed me
> Now would rip me
> From my mother's limbs, sending me
> Tumbling down to be trodden under foot
> Raked, piled, leaped upon in childhood's delight
> Gathered and burned
> The wind will aid a few in escape
> But all such evasion an illusion
> For the decree is quite simple: New leaves from old.

Now, it is my turn
Behold, I am coming
Let all the earth rejoice.

REFERENCES

Addams, Jane. *Democracy and Social Ethics.* Champaign: University of Illinois Press, 1902.

Arendt, Hannah. *Eichmann in Jerusalem: A Report on the Banality of Evil.* New York: Penguin Books, 1963/1977.

Badgett, M. V. Lee. *The Public Professor: How to Use Your Research to Change the World.* New York: New York University Press, 2016.

Berger, John. *Ways of Seeing.* London: BBC and Penguin Books, 1985.

Bondurant, Joan V. *Conquest of Violence.* Berkeley: University of California Press, 1965.

Boorstin, Daniel. *The Image: A Guide to Pseudo-Events in America.* New York: Harper & Row, 1961. Burawoy, Michael. "For Public Sociology." *American Sociological Review* 70 (1), 2005: 4-28.

———. "Open Letter to C. Wright Mills," *Antipode,* 40 (3), 2008, 365-375.

Busch, Lawrence. "Macrosocial Change in Historical Perspective: An Analysis of Epochs." Unpublished Doctoral Dissertation. Ithaca, New York: Cornell University, 1974.

———. "A Tentative Guide to Constructing the Future: Self-Conscious Millenarianism." *Sociological Practice* 1 (Spring 1976): 27-39.

Calderone, Ana. "The Ride of a Lifetime," *Mental Health.* New York: Meredith Corporation, 2018: 22-27.

Carroll, Lewis. *Alice's Adventures in Wonderland.* New York: Dover Thrift, 1865/1993.

Conant, Douglas, and Mette Norgaard. *Touchpoints: Creating Powerful Leadership Connections in the Smallest of Moments.* Hoboken, New Jersey: Jossey-Bass, 2011.

Conrad, Joseph. *Lord Jim.* Peterborough, Ontario: Broadmen Press, 2000. Davies, James C. *When Men Revolt and Why.* New York: Free Press, 1971.

Deming, W. Edwards. *The New Economics for Industry, Government, Education,* 2nd ed. Cambridge, Mass.: MIT Press, 2000.

Dewey, John. *Reconstruction in Philosophy.* Boston: Beacon Press, 1920/1948. Dickens, Charles. *A Christmas Carol.* New York: Dover, 1843/1991.

Dolgon, Corey. *Kill It to Save It: An Autopsy of Capitalism's Triumph over Democracy.* Chicago: Polity Press, 2017.

Durkheim, Emile. *Suicide.* New York: Free Press, 1897/1951.

Emerson, Ralph Waldo. "Nature," in *The Essential Writings of Ralph Waldo Emerson.* New York: Modern Library, 1836/2000: 3-39.

Farson, Richard E. "Why Good Marriages Fail," in Roland Warren (ed.), *New Perspectives on the American Community,* 3rd ed. Chicago: Rand McNally, 1977: 201-217.

Freire, Paolo. *Pedagogy of the Oppressed.* New York: Herder and Herder, 2000.

Fromm, Erich. *Man For Himself: An Inquiry into the Psychology of Ethics.* New York: Holt, Rinehart and Winston, 1947/1976.

Fuller, Robert W. *Somebodies and Nobodies: Overcoming the Abuse of Rank.* Gabriola Island, Canada: New Society Publishers, 2003.

———. *All Rise: Somebodies, Nobodies, and the Politics of Dignity.* San Francisco: Berrett-Koehler, 2006.

Giddens, Anthony. *The Constitution of Society: Outline of the Theory of Structuration.* Cambridge: Polity Press, 1984.

Gould, Stephen Jay. *The Mismeasure of Man.* New York: Norton, 1981.

Gouldner, Alvin W. *The Coming Crisis of Western Sociology.* New York: Basic Books, 1970. Gramsci, Antonio. *Prison Notebooks.* New York: International Publishers, 1971.

Gurr, Ted. *Why Men Rebel.* Princeton: Princeton University Press, 1970.

Haney, C., Banks, W. C., and Zimbardo, P. C. "A Study of Prisoners and Guards in a Simulated Prison," *Naval Research Review,* 1973: 30, 4-17.

Habermas, Jurgen. *The Theory of Communicative Action,* Volumes 1 and 2. Boston: Beacon Press, 1981.

Hayakawa, Samuel I. *Language in Thought and Action.* New York: Harcourt, Brace, & World, 1949.

Hibel, Edna, "Edna Hibel: Conversations," in Plotkin, Theodore (ed.). *Paintings of Edna Hibel*, Mangonia Park, Florida: JAR Publishers, 1974.

Homans, George C. "Bringing Men Back In," *American Sociological Review,* 29, 5 December 1964: 809-818.

Horney, Karen. *The Neurotic Personality of Our Time.* New York: Norton, 1937. Illich, Ivan. *Deschooling Society.* New York: Harper & Row, 1972.

Janis, Irving L., and Daniel Katz. "The Reduction of Intergroup Hostility," *Journal of Conflict Resolution* 3 (March 1959), 85-100.

Johansson, Frans. *The Medici Effect: What Elephants and Epidemics Can Teach Us about Innovation.* Boston: Harvard Business School Press, 2006.

Johnson, John W. "Brandeis Brief." in Hall, Kermit (ed.). *The Oxford Companion to the Supreme Court of the United States.* New York: Oxford University Press.

Jung, Carl G. *The Undiscovered Self.* New York: Signet, 1957/2006.

Kaplan, Abraham. *The New World of Philosophy.* New York: Random House, 1961.

Kelly, George A. *A Theory of Personality: The Psychology of Personal Constructs.* New York: W. W. Norton, 1963.

Kincaid, Harold, *Value-Free Science? Ideals and Illusions.* John Dupre and Alison Wylie (eds.). Oxford: Oxford University Press, 2007.

Knottnerus, J. David, and Bernard Phillips, (eds.). *Bureaucratic Culture and Escalating World Problems: Advancing the Sociological Imagination.* Boulder, Colorado: Paradigm Publishers, 2009.

Knowles, Elizabeth (ed.) *The Oxford Dictionary of Quotations*, 6th ed., Oxford: Oxford University Press, 2004, 3/18: Jane Addams, *Democracy and Social Ethics*, 1902.

Korzybski, Alfred. *Science and Sanity.* Garden City, New York: Country Life Press, 1933.

Leichsenring, Falk, and Sven Rabung. "Effectiveness of Long-Term Psychodynamic Psychotherapy: A Meta-analysis," *JAMA*, 300, October 2008: 1551-1565.

Levin, Jack. "The Influence of Social Frame of Reference for Goal Fulfillment on Social Aggression." Unpublished Ph.D. Dissertation. Boston: Boston University, 1968. See also Phillips and Christner, 2012, op. cit.: 137-139.

Luft, Aliza. "Toward a Dynamic Theory of Action at the Micro Level of Genocide: Killing, Desistance, and Saving in 1994 Rwanda," *Sociological Theory* 33 (2), 2015: 148-172.

Marx, Karl. *Early Writings: Selected Writings in Sociology and Social Philosophy.* T.B. Bottomore and Maximilian Rubel (eds), T. B. Bottomore (tr.). New York: McGraw-Hill, 1844/1964. Masaaki, Imai. *Kaizen: The Key to Japan's Competitive Success.* New York: McGraw-Hill/Irwin, 1986.

Maslow, Abraham. *The Further Reaches of Human Nature.* New York: Viking, 1971.

McQuarie, Donald. "Utopia and Transcendence," *Journal of Popular Culture* 14, (Fall 1980): 242-250. Merton, Robert K. "The Unanticipated Consequences of Purposive Social Action," *American Sociological Review,* 1 (December 1936), 894-904.

Milgram, Stanley. *Obedience to Authority.* New York: Harper & Row, 1974.

Miller, S. M., and Anthony J. Savoie. *Respect and Rights: Class, Race and Gender Today.* Lanham, Maryland: Rowman & Littlefield, 2002.

Mills, C. Wright. *The Sociological Imagination.* New York: Oxford University Press, 1959/2000.

———. *The Causes of World War III.* New York: Simon & Schuster, 1958.

Nisbett, Richard E. *Intelligence and How to Get It: Why Schools and Culture Count.* New York: W. W. Norton, 2009.

O'Hara, John. *Appointment in Samarra.* New York: Vintage Books, 1934/2008.

Ong, Walter J. *Orality and Literacy: The Technologizing of the Word.* London and New York: Methuen, 1982.

Ouspensky, P. D. *The Fourth Way: A Record of Talks and Answers to Questions Based on the Teaching of G. I. Gurdjieff.* New York: Vintage, 1971.

Pearson, Elizabeth, et al. "How Comparative Historical Sociology Can Save the World." in *Trajectories: Newsletter of the ASA Comparative and Historical Sociology Section,* 27 (3), 2016: 1-32.

Peirce, Charles S. "The Fixation of Belief," in Peirce, Charles S., *Philosophical Writings of Peirce.* New York: Dover, 1877/1955, 5–22.

———. "The Scientific Attitude and Fallibilism," in Peirce, Charles S., *Philosophical Writings of Peirce.* New York: Dover, 1896/1955, 42–59.

Pettigrew, Thomas F., Linda R. Tropp, "A Meta-analytic Test of Intergroup Contact Theory," *Journal of Personality and Social Psychology,* 90 (5): 751-783.

Phillips, Bernard. "Expected Value Deprivation and Occupational Preference," *Sociometry* 27 (June 1964): 151-160.

———. *The Invisible Crisis of Contemporary Society: Reconstructing Sociology's Fundamental Assumptions.* Boulder, Colorado: Paradigm Publishers, 2007.

———. "Sociology's Next Steps?" *Contemporary Sociology,* 48 (4) (July 2019): 382-387.

———. *Understanding Terrorism: Building on the Sociological Imagination.* Boulder, Colorado: Paradigm Publishers, 2007.

———. *Worlds of the Future: Exercises in the Sociological Imagination.* Columbus, Ohio: Charles E. Merrill, 1972.

Phillips, Bernard, and David Christner. *Revolution in the Social Sciences: Beyond Control Freaks, Conformity, and Tunnel Vision.* Lanham, Maryland: Lexington Books, 2012: xiv.

Phillips, Bernard, Harold Kincaid and Thomas J. Scheff (eds.). *Toward a Sociological Imagination: Bridging Specialized Fields.* Lanham, Maryland: University Press of America, 2002.

Piketty, Thomas. *Capital in the Twenty-First Century.* Cambridge, Mass.: Harvard University Press, 2014.

Pirsig, Robert M. *Zen and the Art of Motorcycle Maintenance: An Inquiry into Values.* New York, NY: William Morrow and Company, 1974.

Plotkin, Andy. "The Role of the Individual in the Evolution of Post-Bureaucratic Organizations: From a Devolutionary Toward a Post-Bureaucratic Society," *Contemporary Social Sciences,* 25 (1), Jan-Mar, 2016: 59-86.

———. "Toward the Measurement of Paradigms." Unpublished Ph.D. Dissertation. Boston: Boston University, 1977.

Polak, Fred L. *The Image of the Future,* 2 vols. Leyden: W. W. Sythoff, 1961.

———. *The Image of the Future.* San Francisco: Jossey-Bass, 1973.

Prasad, Monica. "Problem-Solving Sociology," *Contemporary Sociology* 47 (4), July 2018: 393-398.

Rauschenbusch, Hilmar S. *Man's Past: Man's Future.* New York: Delacorte, 1969.

Reckwitz, Andreas. *The Invention of Creativity: Modern Society and the Culture of the New.* Malden, Mass.: Polity, 2017.

Reich, Robert B. *Saving Capitalism For the Many, Not the Few.* New York: Vintage Books, 2016.

Romero, Mary. *Introducing Intersectionality.* Medford, Mass.: Polity Press, 2018.

Rosenthal, Robert, and Lenore Jacobson. *Pygmalion in the Classroom.* New York: Holt, Rinehart and Winston, 1968.

Runciman, W. G. *Relative Deprivation and Social Justice.* Berkeley: California University Press, 1966.

Scheff, Thomas J. *Bloody Revenge: Emotions, Nationalism, and War.* Boulder, Colorado: Westview, 1994.

Schumacher, E. F. *Small Is Beautiful: Economics as if People Mattered.* New York: Harper & Row, 1973: 12, 52, 86.

Seidman, Carla. "'Book' of Dialogue at Library," *Sarasota Herald-Tribune,* January 11, 2018: B1, B6.

Shenk, David. *The Genius in All of Us: Why Everything You've Been Told About Genetics, Talent, and IQ Is Wrong.* New York: Doubleday, 2010.

Simmel, Georg. "Metropolis and Mental Life," in *Georg Simmel on Individuality and Social Forms*, Donald N. Levine (ed.). Chicago: University of Chicago Press, 1903/1971: 324-339.

Skockpol, Theda. *States and Social Revolutions*. Cambridge: Cambridge University Press, 1979.

Stein, Arlene, and Jessie Daniels. *Going Public: A Guide for Social Scientists*. Chicago: University of Chicago Press, 2017.

Sternheimer, Karen. *The Social Scientist's Soapbox: Adventures in Writing Public Sociology*. New York: Routledge, 2017.

Sztompka, Piotr. *The Sociology of Social Change*. Cambridge, Mass.: Blackwell Publishers, 1994. Thompson, Larry. "Creativity Holds Key to Success," *Sarasota Herald-Tribune*, October 6, 2017. *Time* magazine, April 29/May 6, 2019: 1-140.

Turner, Jonathan H. "The Social Psychology of Terrorism," in Bernard Phillips (ed.), *Understanding Terrorism: Building on the Sociological Imagination*, Boulder, Colorado: Paradigm Publishers, 2007: 115-145.

Van Vogt, A. E. *The World of Null-A*. New York: Berkley Publishing, 1945/1970.

———. *The Players of Null-A*. New York: Berkley Publishing, 1948.

Vidich, Arthur J., and Joseph Bensman. *Small Town in Mass Society: Class, Power, and Religion in a Rural Community*. Garden City, New York: Doubleday, 1960.

Wade, Lisa. *American Hookup: The New Culture of Sex on Campus*. New York: Norton, 2017.

Watts, Duncan J. "Should Social Science be More Solution-Oriented?" *Nature Human Behaviour* 1, 2017: 1-4.

Weber, Max. *Economy and Society*. Oakland: University of California Press, 1922/2013.

———. *The Protestant Ethic and the Spirit of Capitalism*. New York: Scribner, 1958. Whitman, Walt. *Leaves of Grass*. New York: Random House, 1892/2004.

Williams, Robin M., Jr. "Major Value Orientations in America," *American Society*. New York: Knopf, 1970: 452–500.

Wrong, Dennis H. "The Oversocialized Concept of Man in Modern Sociology," *American Sociological Review* 26 (2), April 1961: 183-193.

INDEX

Addams, Jane, 11, 15, 131
addiction, 105
Adorno, Theodor, xii
Allyson, June, 52
Alumkal, Antony, 104
Anderson, Hans Christian, 65, 74
Anthony, Marc, 27
Anthony, Susan B., 92
Arendt, Hannah, 8
Astaire, Fred, 52
Atwood, Margaret, 25

Bach, Richard, 124
Badgett, M. V. Lee, 10
Banks, W. C., 113-114
Beale, Howard, 60
Bebel, August, 72
Becket, Thomas, 3
Bellamy, Edward, 72
Bensman, Joseph, 77-79, 104
Bergen, Edgar, 137-138
Berger, John, 33-34, 75
Blake, William, 136
Bondurant, Joan V., 119-121
Boorstin, Daniel, 75
Bourdain, Anthony, 106-107
Bourdieu, Pierre, xii
Bradbury, Ray, 25
Brandeis, Louis C., 41-43, 60
Browning, Robert, 12, 86
Buddha, 67-69, 71, 76, 83-84, 102, 104
Buddhist economics, 56
Bulletin of the Atomic Scientists, 21
Burawoy, Michael, xii, 10, 43
Bureaucracy, 4, 6, 29, 40, 56
Burgess, Anthony, 25
Busch, Lawrence, 40-41
Bush, George H. W., 22

Calderone, Ana, 106-107
Camus, Albert, 92, 140

Fuller, Robert W., 87
Funakoshi, Gichin, 10, 30

Gandhi, Mahatma, 119-121
Garland, Judy, 52
Giddens, Anthony, xii, 10
Golding, William, 36
Gould, Stephen J., 12, 49
Gouldner, Alvin, x-xi, 43-45
gradation, 47-48
Gramsci, Antonio, xii, 25, 97, 102
Gronlund, Laurence, 72
Green, Adolph, 53
Gurdjieff, George, 30, 102
Gurr, Ted, 69

Habermas, Jurgen, xii, 10
Hamlet, 27, 30
Haney, C., 113-114
Harrison, George, 142
Henley, William Ernest, 130-132
Hayakawa, Samuel I., 46
Hearst, William Randolph, 68
Hibel, Edna, 86
Hitler, Adolph, 27, 46, 94
Holocaust, 8
Homans, George C., 44-45
Horkheimer, Max, xii
Horne, Lena, 52
Horney, Karen, x, 70-71
Huxley, Aldous, x, 25

Illich, Ivan, 32-33
invisible crisis, 69

Jacobsen, Lenore, 12
Janis, Irving L., 120
Johansson, Frans, 52-53, 55
Jong-un, Kim, 8
Jung, Carl G., 10, 77

kaizen, 13-15, 28, 102
Katz, Daniel, 120
Keller, Helen, 45-46, 133
Kelly, Gene, 52

Turner, Jonathan H., ix-xv, 93-94, 96

unanticipated consequences, 26-27

value neutrality, 88-89
Van Vogt, A. E., 46, 48
Verdi, Giuseppe, 49
Vidich, Arthur J., 77-79, 104
Voltaire, 10
Vonnegut, Kurt, 25

Wade, Lisa, 80
Walesa, Lech, 92
Warren, Earl, 43
Watts, Duncan J. 43
Weber, Max, ix, 22-24, 79, 113
Weiss, Neil, 2-3, 90, 93, 135
Wells, H. G., 72
Welles, Orson, 68
Whitman, Walt, 51-52
Williams, Esther, 52
Wright, Eric Olin, xii
Wrong, Dennis H., 44-45

Zimbardo, Philip, 113-114

About the Authors

Bernard Phillips, with a BA from Columbia, an MA from Washington State U and a PhD from Cornell, has been a sociology professor at the U of North Carolina, the U of Illinois and Boston U. He co-founded the Section on Sociological Practice of the American Sociological Association and founded and directed "The Sociological Imagination Group." Annual meetings yielded 3 volumes of 30 research papers that he edited. He has taught, consulted or done research at the U oft Skopje (Yugoslavia), the Puerto Rico Department of Education, the Japan Center for Area Development, Florida State U and the U of Hawaii, and has published 20 books on such topics as social research, terrorism, and constructing the future. He continues to be inspired by the interdisciplinary vision of C. Wright Mills, his mentor at Columbia, whose *The Sociological Imagination* was rated the second most influential book for sociologists published during the entire 20th century.

Thomas J. Savage holds a BA from the U of Redlands, California, and a Master of Divinity and Master of Sacred Theology Degree from the Boston U School of Theology. He served as an ordained minister for 25 years, a sheriff's lieutenant for 23 years, and is a world traveler to 89 countries. He created a unique experiment in community policing, with over ten thousand volunteers for a citizen patrol. He founded and directs the Sarasota Public Arts Fund, serves on the Ringling College Scholarship Committee, and is a significant supporter for cultural and philanthropic causes.

Andy Plotkin, with a BA, MS and Ph.D. from Boston University, has taught and tutored students in sociology, criminology, communications, and English in many universities. He has focused his writing on understanding the intersection of the humanities, the social sciences, and the biophysical sciences as a basis for solving society's most pressing problems.

Neil S. Weiss holds a BBA (Accounting, Magna Cum Laude) and MBA (Statistics, First in class) from Baruch College, and a PhD (Business) from Columbia U, as well as a professional CPA license. He has worked as an accountant and an auditor, and has taught at Baruch College, Pace U, Montclair State U, Northwood U, Strayer U, and Columbia U (Associate Professor). In addition, he has conducted training programs in accounting and financial statement analysis for banks throughout the world. A key article of his is "The statement of cash flows--problems with current rules," *CPA Journal*, 2007.

Max O. Spitzer is by far the youngest author. He was attracted to sociology by Andy Plotkin. Beginning with Mills and then Phillips and Plotkin, he represents a fourth generations pointing in Mills' interdisciplinary direction. His background is in science, medicine and sociology. He sees this knowledge as most useful for addressing many of the unsolved and highly threatening problems of our times. Following Theodore Roosevelt's vision, he is anxious to "enter the arena" where present efforts to confront current problems are failing us, and to use broad understanding to make progress on them.

Lightning Source UK Ltd.
Milton Keynes UK
UKHW012036030320
359722UK00003B/47